GlobalSolutions for Teams

Moving from Collision to Collaboration

Sylvia B. Odenwald

IRWIN
Professional Publishing

Chicago • Bogotá • Boston • Buenos Aires • Caracas
London • Madrid • Mexico City • Sydney • Toronto

Senior sponsoring editor:	Cynthia A. Zigmund
Marketing manager:	Kelly Sheridan
Project editor:	Jane Lightell
Production supervisor:	Lara Feinberg
Senior designer:	Larry J. Cope
Typeface:	11/13 Times Roman
Printer:	Quebecor Book Press

ISBN: 0-7863-0476-6

Printed in the United States of America
1 2 3 4 5 6 7 8 9 0 QBP 2 1 0 9 8 7 6 5

This book is dedicated to our teams of worldwide associates and clients who collaborate daily on GlobalSolutions.

Author's Note

Believing that tenets must be practiced and tested, we developed a unique corporate culture for The Odenwald Connection. The ideas evolved from our diverse corporate and consulting experience as we realized that:

- Each client project required a totally different proposal and process.
- The expertise needed to solve corporate client problems required an *outside the box* approach for our firm.
- Multinational projects most often moved through three stages: (1) collision, (2) coexistence, and (3) collaboration.

DIVERSE CORPORATE CLIENT PROJECTS

The needs of client companies were changing dramatically, and the solutions to those challenges were so diverse that no longer could we design program modules that could be used again and again with various client companies. Each situation was significantly different, requiring unique solutions. Project conclusions came through with distinct regularity.

- The majority of our corporate clients had expanded globally or were moving in that direction. With today's mobile workforce, every company employee must be trained to a competency level that will support enough commonality to work on any team in any country anywhere in the world.
- Off-the-shelf training programs simply did not work as client corporations and their customers crossed domestic and international lines.
- Often the solution for a client corporation was not just the training program they requested, but involved a range of solutions from business development to financing structures.

EXPERIENCED CONSULTING TEAMS

Our concept of the 21st Century consulting firm was begun in 1984—a virtual corporation of entrepreneurial consultants with a depth of expertise and the flexibility to create solutions for clients' changing needs. Today's corporations need consultants located in countries around the globe to assist clients with GlobalSolutions for business operations worldwide. Consulting isssues include international business risk assessment, financial engineering, and customized employee training using the culture and language appropriate in each local geographic area.

COLLISION—COEXISTENCE—COLLABORATION

As teams and corporations learn to work together, they move through a three-phase evolution that takes them from individual entities into a workgroup. Without an understanding that their individual cultures and workstyles are diverse, the new relationship will remain on a collision course to nowhere. When the group begins to recognize, admit, and accept the differences, they then move into a collective state of coexistence—*a live and let live* attitude. The last phase—collaboration—is accomplished when the group begins to learn how to negotiate work parameters and accomplish tasks through a willingness to complete the assigned project.

Last year we felt impelled to pass along the evolving processes we are experiencing as we continue to assist clients with GlobalSolutions. So, we formed a kinetic workgroup culture to write this book. Originally, small project groups discussed and worked to develop concepts for the research. Then a Dallas-based core workgroup of The Odenwald Connection formed including: Bill Matheny, Beverly Forte, Mary Jo Beebe, Gayle Watson, Sue Maass, Mary Stoddard, Lynda Coumelis, and Sylvia Odenwald.

From this nucleus, additional units formed for research and specific projects: Peter Beckschi, Serge Ogranovitch, Laree Kiely, Wolf-Dieter Gebhardt, Nessa Loewenthal, Zachary Townsend, Clifford Clarke, Bob Greenleaf, Bob Wright, Chang Young-Chul, Mark de Graaf, J. C. Bemvenutti, Francoise Morissette, Hussein Hammady, Tom Japp, B. J. Chakiris, Don Brush, Kareen Strickler, Zuhlaiha Ismail, Bill Shea, and Zareen Karani Lam de Araoz.

In order to include current data and workgroup experience up to the very last minute before the press deadline, a core alliance production team was formed with Cynthia Zigmund, Jane Lightell, Lynn Holt, Tina Stanislav, and Beverly Forte.

I am indebted to all of these professionals, to client corporations, and to experienced company managers for their insight and contributions to this work.

Sylvia B. Odenwald

Contents

Corporate GlobalSolutions

L os Angeles is accustomed to shocks, but "few have been more jarring than the seismic shifts in the fortunes of L.A. Gear Inc. A smash in the 80s, trendy sneaker maker L.A. Gear crashed in the 90s. New management is betting heavily on the appeal of Americana abroad and new foreign suppliers and distributors."[1] After several false starts, the corporation now accepts what its competitors have long known—you cannot rely on domestic markets alone. International markets are where the action is in the sneaker business. The reason is simple. The United States has about 516 million feet to be covered, and the rest of the world has 11 billion. L.A. Gear acquired distributors in the U.K., Germany, the Netherlands, Belgium, and Luxembourg in 1993, spending over $16 million. The company set up a European headquarters in Amsterdam and formed subsidiaries in France and Italy. L.A. Gear also formed an Asian joint venture with Inchcape PLD, the British marketing firm to help it move into the Pacific Rim market.[2]

U.S. corporations are presented with a tempting array of global markets in which to expand their businesses. In the early 1990s, international companies concentrated on business development opportunities in the European Union until EU collaboration hit some major barriers. Southeast Asia then emerged as the favored market for global expansion. In 1993 Mexico and Canada came into focus with the North American Free Trade Agreement. Following the signing of NAFTA, free-market reforms and economic revivals have U.S. corporations flocking to invest in Latin America.

For example, Coca-Cola is investing $800 million to protect its already sizable stake in Brazil, while PepsiCo Inc. is spending $300 million to break into that market. Procter & Gamble Company is investing heavily in Latin America—$800 million in the past five years. P&G receives eight percent of its total revenue from this region.[3] Energy companies are also interested in the Latin American market. Tenneco Gas Company as a partner with other private companies and Brazil's state-run Petrobras has proposed a massive natural-gas pipeline network that will stretch from Brazil to Bolivia, Peru, Argentina, and eventually over the Andes into Chile. Houston-based Enron Corporation is a partner with YPFB, the Bolivian state-run oil company, for the Bolivian section of the pipeline.[4]

Trade, telecommunications, and transport ministers are forging a Free Trade Agreement of the Americas (FTAA) through steps to pull together the hemisphere's existing free-trade blocs. The ultimate goal is to mold free-trade alliances in the hemisphere, such as Mercosur, the Andean Pact, and the North American Free Trade Agreement, into a web of commerce. The region is the fastest-growing U.S. export market, taking almost $90 billion worth of U.S. goods in 1994. By the year 2000, the Commerce Department estimates that the region will surpass Europe as a customer for U.S. wares. By 2010, it will surpass the combined markets of Europe and Japan.

CURRENT INTERNATIONAL CHALLENGES

In 1990 The Odenwald Connection conducted a study of what corporations were doing to train employees to work in the global marketplace. *Global Training: How to Design a Program for the Multinational Corporation* related the results of the study and outlined a process for the development and implementation of a training strategy that provides direction for global organizations.

As a result of these findings, ongoing consulting projects, and current research, we have uncovered startling approaches used by many international companies. These corporations are plunging into international markets like giants in a doll house. They add new workers, expand into new markets, and declare business as usual—continuing as they have done in the past. They most often assume that what has worked successfully for them domestically in product and service development, sales, marketing, and customer service will also work anywhere in the world. So a surprising number of well-intentioned companies are launching into the international arena under the assumption that if something plays in Indianapolis, it will probably play in Istanbul. Or if it works in Brussels, it will be successful in Buenos Aires. Nothing could be further from the truth—or more costly to the global corporation.

For example, when $300 million Standard Microsystems Corporation first ventured into global competition, it saw no reason to change its networking products for the European market. "Initially, our attitude was shopping the U.S. product outside the U.S.," admits Lance Murrah, vice president of marketing at Hauppauge, New York-based SMS.[5] However, company management quickly ran into problems. They found that their American packaging violated certain environmental laws in Europe. The labels, printed in English, needed to be printed in five other languages to meet local customer needs. Fortunately, they were able to learn from their mistakes. In 1993 their international sales accounted for 45 percent of total revenues.

"In fact, the inability of U.S. companies to compete in world markets as well as they should is still very much their own doing," says Edward Mervosh, editor-in-chief of *International Business*. In the majority of U.S. companies, Mervosh points out that:

> Senior managers . . . are still incredibly provincial in their outlook, clinging to the notion that the home market is the beginning and end of business. More disconcerting is that many who are aware of the importance of going international don't understand that foreign business is different from domestic business. Too many multinationals mistakenly think doing business abroad is simply an extension of doing business at home. Too few U.S. multinationals take the time to select and train their executives carefully for critical expatriate positions that ultimately will determine whether their international strategies succeed or fail.[6]

Although multinational corporations with headquarters outside the United States are more aware of cultural differences, they too are not always certain that their expansion plans and policies will work with partnerships outside their base-country or within the American market.

As we consult with corporations on GlobalSolutions, we find that most of the barriers they face are from flaws in their global business development and personnel selection. Implemented solutions may involve negotiations with national government decision makers on tariffs, laws, and regulations. Other answers may be redesigning a service to fit the area's customer needs, selecting a national product name and promoting it through appropriate advertising and marketing channels, or getting work done with a intercultural workforce located in many geographic areas.

CAREFULLY PLAN EXPANSION

Experience teaches us that it is much easier to carefully plan expansion into a new geographic market with culturally attuned employees than it is to recover after failure in that market has occurred. To change customers' perception of a company and its employees is much more difficult than it is to initially introduce corporate products and people into a new region with an appropriate strategic plan and selection process. Image and acceptance are essential to success in international markets.

GLOBAL BUSINESS DEVELOPMENT

Doing business transnationally is never easy. Added to domestic business issues are international factors of operating over geographical distances and time zones, fluctuating currencies, differences in customs and language, legal variations, and constantly shifting economic and political issues. With these points in mind, how do corporate executives select which countries to move into and determine appropriate marketing, once they have decided to expand into international markets?

One of the yardsticks popularly used for business development is the per capita income of targeted countries, without any seasoned consideration of the addressability of the market, current distribution systems, and crucial cultural considerations. Result: expensive but unnecessary failures and pull-outs.

One current example of the error of using per capita income as an operative in deciding international marketing strategy is provided by a leading American plastic products manufacturer who selected France and Spain as deserving target markets for its products. The excellence of the company's products is undisputed. But the firm failed to see that the conservative French and Spanish homemakers (48 million) simply do not like plastic, which they culturally view as second-class storage material. They prefer metal and porcelain products. And since they can afford to buy them, they disdain the plastic and turn their collective back on them.

On the other hand, the 55 million newly freed homemakers of the nine Eastern European countries are less pretentious, less able to afford metal and porcelain, and literally adore the affordable, lightweight plastic products. Hence the American company's products would be in greater demand in Eastern Europe, where they would also produce higher profits and a corner on the market much more quickly. This highly successful U.S. company is reluctant to face a *provable cultural fact* that could cost them millions of dollars in lost sales in Europe.

New and different strategies must be implemented for a company to be successful in the global marketplace. Mars Inc. is an example of a company whose time-honored methods are not working. Hershey Foods Corporation in particular is ahead of Mars with new-product innovation and marketing. With aggressive marketing and acquisitions, Hershey is increasing both its marketshare and profits in a flat market.[7] Mars has also lost marketshare in Western Europe, and clearly needs a new global perspective.

Other companies now experiencing massive problems, loss of global marketshare, and downward profits are using quick-fix approaches to correct their direction. They invest millions of dollars to implement total quality management (TQM) and reengineering programs. Too late they discover that even reengineering will not surface needed solutions, unless focus is centered on the impact of intercultural differences.

McDonald's inadvertently offended thousands of Muslims by printing a Koran scripture on two million throwaway hamburger bags for takeout orders of children's Happy Meals. This stir was caused by the world's leading fast food chain in a World Cup promotion that featured flags of the 24 competitors in the summer 1994 soccer championship. The green and white flag of Saudi Arabia, contains an Arabic passage that can be translated as "There is no God but Allah, and Mohammed is his Prophet," sacred words that Muslims say should not be crumpled up and thrown in the trash.[8] This incident shows the potential pitfalls faced by multinational corporations that do not do their homework before offering products to millions of people from different countries.

GLOBALTHINK

Old ways do not work in the rush to globalization. The message is clear: companies and the people in them must change to *GlobalThink*.

GlobalThink begins with a global mindset. It is thinking about the global marketplace through a worldwide perspective about alliances, potential markets, new products, and new technologies. GlobalThink includes flexibility, a willingness to accept and work in a world of change, complexity, and conflict. It also includes the courage to takes risks—to make paradigm shifts from the strategies and processes that have worked in the past and to visualize and implement innovative new methods.

Corporations are seeking executives who exemplify GlobalThink. Hugo Boss AG, one of the world's largest makers of men's fashions, found just such a leader in Peter Littmann. Not only was Littmann from a different business, but he was born and educated in what was once Czechoslovakia. Why did the board choose someone who had no experience in the men's clothing business? They were looking for someone with professional executive skills who could lead a large growing international company and who would bring innovative, creative ideas to their business. Prior to moving to Hugo Boss, Littmann was running a large international carpet company. "The carpet business is very difficult, very competitive," he says, "because it is a commodity business. If you have a good idea in design in the carpet business your competition is copying your idea in 24 hours."[9] Littmann thought of having famous artists design their carpets which would allow them new creative designs, copyright the designs, and present a new selling strategy. Littmann was asked to run the German subsidiary of Marzotto, the giant Italian textile manufacturer, and immediately made a big name for himself by revolutionizing the company's product line overnight. "What's more, he took Hugo Boss in a bold new direction at a time when the company was still doing very well and its big markets were weak."[10] He changed the company's organizational structure from a pyramid to a flatter organization to drive decision making down to a lower level. Littmann sees his CEO role as a coach who gives people a chance to do their job and supports them in it.

Marketing and business development executives must also use *GlobalThink* and become familiar with global business development basics. Using a cultural viewpoint, they should answer these basic corporate questions as they move into new global markets:

- How do you decide the best countries for your firm?
- Once the decision is made on sound principles, how do you keep the company focused?
- How do you measure success? (HINT: Not by the bottom line—but by *customer satisfaction,* which virtually guarantees return on equity and return on assets)

TARGETED PERSONNEL SELECTION AND TRAINING

After the business questions are answered and development strategies are in place, the next questions for corporate consideration are:

- *Who* should be sent to the new market area?
- And what tools should you give them to do the job?

Professional development and cross-cultural training are crucial for success in the global marketplace. However, many corporations believe that one training course can solve all of their inadequacies. Before a training program can be designed and presented, rigorous personnel selection processes should be thought through and put into place.

The selection of executives for multinational corporations of the 21st Century will be based on quite different competencies. "What they're looking for is not only technical knowledge but a global perspective," notes Fortunat Mueller-Maerki, a partner at Egon Zehnder International, an executive search firm based in New York City. Executives like Michael H. Spindler (CEO of Apple Computer), Eckhard Pfeiffer (CEO of Compaq) and Lodewijk J. R. de Vink (chief operating officer of Warner-Lambert Co.) are citizens of the world. They are, in many ways, cultural chameleons. When in the U.S., they look, act, and, in some cases, even sound like Americans. But they have an additional dimension to their experience and way of thinking.

The thrust behind this rising tide of *inpatriates*, as they are coming to be called, is no secret to personnel experts. The global pool of executives with multicultural skills—and quite often with U.S. education and business experience—is expanding even as the American pool virtually stagnates. That stagnation results from the decision of many U.S. companies to cut back on the costly business of sending their own people abroad and filling most senior executive slots at non-U.S. subsidiaries with locals.[11]

Although it may not be listed on résumés, endurance is one quality that makes executives successful in the new round-the-clock global economy. Take business travel, for example. Spending on international travel by U.S. businesses has increased by about two-thirds since 1990, as indicated by a recent survey of 1,447 companies by American Express.[12] With cellular phones, fax machines, modems, and laptops, managers can work round-the-clock, connected to any place in the world. Downtime, even in the middle of the night, is a thing of the past. On top of that, in the corporate downsized world, managers are working harder to take up the slack. They really have little choice. "They have to run with the staminacs," writes Lee Smith in *Fortune*.[13]

However, the good news is that even if this is not executives' *modus operandi*, they can take steps to increase their stamina. If they are extroverts, they have a head start. Also, Smith suggests that they can reduce the number of hours of sleep to six or so and at the same time increase their energy level. The secrets are diet, exercise, and attitude.

Joaquin R. Carbanel III is an example of the new executive globe trotter. Carbanel, 42, president of BellSouth Europe states, "You've got to be adaptive . . . . And you can't stand still." To win an Israeli cellular service contract, Carbanel logged three trips from Atlanta to Tel Aviv in four months. At 16 hours a flight, "it's murder." But it's not unusual. "You must be incredibly hardy, able to withstand a lot of time zones."[14]

Carbanel constantly adapts his business style to the cultural environment *du jour*—from Latin America's low-key social wooing, to the in-your-face negotiations that are needed in Israel, to Australia's laid-back ways. Luckily, he confides, after a few years as a global manager, "you feel at home wherever you are." For global executives, that goes with the territory.

CHANGING SUCCESS CRITERIA

The criteria for a corporation's success is also changing. In the 1980s, *In Search of Excellence* was a mega-bestselling business book. Authors Thomas J. Peters and Robert H. Waterman Jr. chose America's 31 best companies for this work. More than 1 million hardbound copies were printed, and publishers scrambled for more books on the secrets of business success. In 1994 Graef S. Crystal decided to calculate "how an investor would have fared had he followed the prescriptions of the two eminent management doctors and constructed a portfolio consisting of equal investments in each of the 31 companies." He concluded that the faithful adherent to the Peters-Waterman thesis would have earned much less than by simply tossing the money into a fund tied to the Standard & Poor's 500. "I wonder if we have really yet figured out what produces a company's long-term success," Mr. Crystal said.[15]

Since Peters and Waterman were looking at internal corporate processes and their impact, an investment portfolio comparison may be stretching a point. However, it does emphasize the fact that companies are struggling to remain successful while learning the new aspects of the global economy.

Managing fast international growth is difficult enough for large corporations. As managers of middle-market companies are discovering, the complexities and skills needed to succeed rise exponentially when they start doing business internationally. For along with the acceleration in global business come even bigger management problems. "Managing rapid international growth is akin to trying to speed safely each day along a different highway—with road signs in different languages and traffic laws that may or may not require you to drive on the opposite side of the road," writes Gregory L. Miles.[16]

Some leading management experts question whether U.S. midsize companies can manage breakneck foreign growth. "[U.S. companies'] ability to conceive global strategies far exceeds their ability to execute them," argues Jay R. Galbraith, a widely published management expert at the Center for Effective Organizations at the University of Southern California.[17] Too often, he says, U.S. companies of any size underestimate cultural problems involved in selling overseas, as well as the kind of after-sales customer service and product distribution needed to build and hold marketshare.

This is particularly true of midsize corporations, argues Christopher A. Bartlett, a management expert at Harvard Business School who is doing research at INSEAD, one of Europe's leading management schools, in Fontainebleau, France. "Can midsize companies manage rapid international growth?" asks Mr. Bartlett, author of *Managing Across Borders: The Transnational Solution.* "For most companies the answer will be no. There's a mismatch between resources and the rate of growth. Midsize companies have insufficient numbers of managers and will exceed their ability to implement strategies. But companies will keep increasing their strategic stake. It will take a disaster for them to slow down."[18]

One egregious—but by no means uncommon—case is biotech company Centocor Inc., whose overly rapid, misguided foreign expansion helped inflict staggering losses over five years. "It almost sank the whole ship," says president and CEO David P. Holveck, who saved the company with drastic restructuring after taking the helm in November 1992."[19]

Global competition is so fierce that U.S. companies must go abroad to learn to compete and to build up size so they can survive. "There's a much shorter time window for establishing yourself in new markets," says George S. Yip, a professor at UCLA's John E. Anderson Graduate School of Management and author of *Total Global Strategy.* "If you don't do it, another company will."[20]

"Few companies can maintain healthy growth rates year after year without going international," adds Charles R. Joseph, vice president of worldwide field operations for Trimble Navigation Ltd., a maker of super-high-tech navigation technology in Sunnyvale,

California.[21] Trimble is one of many midsize firms embarking on ambitious global growth quests.

For corporations to meet the demands of doing business as global organizations, more is required than just change. Global companies must make clear choices that will lead to transformation. To find GlobalSolutions to their new challenges, they must have VISION:

FIGURE 1

GlobalSolutions

V isionary Leadership
I nnovative Strategies
S ynthesis of Cultures
I ntegration of Teams
O ngoing Flexibility
N ever-Ending Transformation

- **Visionary Leaders** who can create a fluid corporate structure that can respond instantly to changing global needs.
- GlobalVision which encourages implementation of **Innovative Strategies** to create effective teams from diverse cultures to bring timely products to the global marketplace.
- GlobalCulture created from a **Synthesis of Cultures** at the individual, organizational, and societal levels.
- **Integration of Teams** into GlobalWork Teams which combine employees' specific skills into integrated teams at the management and workgroup level.
- Continuing the process of finding new GlobalSolutions by **Ongoing Flexibility** and **Never-Ending Transformation** at every level of the organization.

Corporations must implement this VISION to be successful in today's global marketplace. We can stubbornly cling to the old ways we know best or we can together redesign work into collaborative workgroup cultures. The starting point for these successful ventures must be mutual cultural respect. Then the process can go forward, as individuals collectively explore new ways of working together in GlobalWork Teams to reach company goals.

This book shares ways to develop your company's VISION and highlights how some global companies are currently tackling the challenges of the Transformation Age with their own unique VISION. Chapters 1 and 2 begin this process by addressing the development and transformation of corporate culture through Visionary Leadership. Chapter 3 explores the importance of Innovative Strategies in bringing team members from diverse cultures together to accomplish corporate goals. A model to facilitate the Synthesis of Cultures to move GlobalWork teams from initial phases of collision to productive, collaborative working units is provided in Chapters 4 and 6. Chapter 5 addresses competencies needed by team members in various levels of the organization. The book's final chapter discusses the need for Ongoing Flexibility and Never-Ending Transformation to provide a global competitive edge in the marketplace.

One thing is evident: doing business internationally can expose corporations to all kinds of risks. The ability to successfully manage these changes has become one of the most important factors for the prosperity of global companies. Only corporations who recognize the differences and concentrate on appropriate GlobalSolutions will make the transformations necessary for success in the 21st Century.

Chapter 1

The Age of Transformation

The Age of Transformation

In the midst of conducting business, 20th Century Information Age corporations are transforming into 21st Century global organizations. Just as organizations have moved from the Industrial Revolution into the Information Age, so they are now speeding into the Age of Transformation. This is an era in which information is communicated and work is conducted across borders, cultures, functions, companies, industries, and locations—seemingly *trans-everything*. These new and emerging demands on companies around the world are occurring faster than the speed of sound—breaking not just barriers of speed but the barriers of cyberspace.

The transformation of companies from domestic to global organizations leads to struggles with ever-changing terminology, technologies, and resources. These new organizations require different approaches to leadership, culture, and teamwork. New processes must also be designed for developing products and getting them to market, to the customer, and back again for reengineering and redesign before sending the next versions off the assembly line to repeat the process. The speed with which new processes are actuated also produces new measures of success. No longer are companies ridiculed for a product that fails. They are applauded for their innovation and quick response to needs and trends, and their competitive ratio moves up the scale as they take their new knowledge back to the drawing board for their next entry into the marketplace.

In addition to new ways of developing and marketing products, corporations are finding that transportation is a key component in globalization. Shipping their product to market is also changing.

To meet these new requirements, shippers today have to be more global and multinational. They must provide distribution, supply chain management, and service to customers that span several continents. Federal Express, United Parcel Service, and Emery Worldwide are dealing with these challenges. Their goals are to establish programs for shippers that meet their needs for reliability, customer orientation, and value added service—regardless of the continent or international location.

Many large transportation carriers are now offering a new generation of information technology-logistics programs to improve global distribution. For example, the logistics unit of APC, the large American West Coast steamship and train operator, offers an advanced system blending high-tech hardware and customized software that can, for example, efficiently move thousands of containers ferrying Toys "R" Us products from Asian factories to 900 retail outlets around the world. At the same time, APC's logistics system provides precise, timely information on where every container is at any given time—and what is in it. APC operatives in Asia feed data on product type, color, number of items and destination into computers located at the unit's California computer center. This data is organized and immediately forwarded to Toys "R" Us two weeks before the company's cargo arrives at its destination. This information allows Toys "R" Us—or other APC customers—to reorder missing product, inform their customers of potential delays, and, if necessary, divert cargo en route.[1] In addition to APC, trucker Schneider National Inc., package truck carrier Yellow Corporation, and global transportation conglomerate CSX (owner of steamship giant Sea-Land Service Inc.) are the leading providers of sophisticated information technology-based logistics services.

SIGNS OF TRANSFORMATION

Some corporations are seriously questioning the viability of many concepts and processes they used during the last two decades. These include:

- Highly structured organizations
- Layers of middle management
- Local-only customers and markets
- Top-down decisions
- Business as usual
- Focus on individual skills for work performance
- Large numbers of employees working in company-owned offices
- 8-to-5 work hours
- Corporate culture

NEW CORPORATE PROCESSES

Companies are finding that transformation processes and concepts are essential to their success in the global marketplace. These include:

- Fluid organization styles
- Management by teamwork
- Focusing on *thinking global . . . acting local*
- Bottom-up decisions
- *If it ain't broke, break it* concept
- Emphasis on team competencies and performance
- Lean companies cutting overhead fat by letting employees work at home or from remote locations
- Flex time with project teams from many time zones working around the clock, around the world
- Synthesis of diverse cultures

TRANSFORMATION

To be successful globally, corporations must develop a strategy to structure transformational processes which are flexible enough to adapt to daily changes in employees, customers, products, and services.

In an attempt to manage these transformations, corporations have often spent billions of dollars embracing the latest management fads whether or not they fit their specific company. But incremental change can mask the need for corporate transformation.

"A corporation is a living organism, and it has to continue to shed its skin," states Intel CEO Andy Grove.[2] Corporate methods, focus, and values have to change, and the sum total of those changes is transformation. "One of the biggest lessons I've learned," Grove continues, "is that it is always easier to put strategic changes into action than to declare them a policy."

Transformed Organizational Structures

Over the past two decades, American corporations have cut layers of middle management in a drive to flatten their organizations, reduce their workforce, and delegate more responsibility to workers. They are replacing the pyramid organizational structure of the past with a new horizontal management model.

These corporate trends also are becoming evident outside the United States. European countries are following these changes— particularly Britain, Sweden, Finland, and The Netherlands. Privatized companies such as British Telecommunications PLC and British Airways PLC have led the way by slashing management layers and becoming more entrepreneurial.

Typical of this trend is Sun Life Assurance Society PLC, a Bristol-based insurer managing $24.6 million in assets. In an article, "The New World of Work" (October 17, 1994), *Business Week* reported that:

> Sun Life eliminated most middle management and reorganized once-isolated customer service representatives . . . into teams that handle jobs from start to end. The result: Turnaround time to settle claims was cut nearly in half, while new business grew 45%. But the change is also unsettling. Although team leader Juliette Britton finds work more fulfilling, management cuts mean "there's nowhere else for me to go."[3]

In Japan, attempts to create new work practices are also in their infancy. Toshiba is experimenting with telecommuting for software researchers, while Orix Corporation, Japan's largest leasing company, now hires workers on a short-term basis to build its branch network.

VIRTUAL CORPORATION

Advances in computer and communications technology have spawned the virtual corporation with a new breed of nomadic executives. These executives are not tied to any particular headquarters building or city—their office is where the data port is.

And their ranks are sure to grow as more businesses push to shorten management response time while keeping staff lean. For example, while VeriFone's nominal headquarters are located in Redwood City, California, its executives view their primary meeting place as the company's computer network. VeriFone's CEO has his office in Redwood City but is on the road 80 percent of the time. The senior vice president for operations is located in Los Angeles, the human resources director in Dallas, and the chief information officer in Santa Fe. They meet face-to-face every six weeks to maintain human contact.[4]

TRANSFORMED SOCIETIES

These transformations are also affecting nations and governments, which are struggling with solving trade, economic, education, and military problems to build a world of peace. Old rules of sovereignty and isolationism no longer apply as countries strive to build a new world order.

In the 1800s, the United States was called a *melting pot*, as immigrants from other countries added their cultural identities to America and became citizens. Many strides have been made in understanding and appreciating this diversity. Friendships have been born, communities have been enriched, and teamwork has increased company productivity. These steps forward have occurred through individuals who have opened their minds and expanded their horizons to exchange a self-centered view for a world-centered vision. However, the clock of cultural change moves forward only a few seconds each year. Over one hundred years later, racial tensions and violence are still major problems. Violent acts of terrorists bloody world headlines of both electronic and print media.

Darryl Hartley-Leonard, chairman of Hyatt Hotels Corporation, knows that when news about crime is broadcast nationally and internationally, tourists and business travelers avoid those cities where the acts of violence occurred. Recognizing the negative impact that these social problems have on the corporate bottom line, Hartley-Leonard and Hyatt have taken a proactive role in finding solutions. "No longer can we hide from the social, educational, and cultural challenges taking place in this country. How we deal with them will shape how we work and live, how our companies do or do not prosper, and how our families do or do not thrive as we move into the next century." (Reprinted from a paid advertising section prepared for the November 2, 1992 issue of FORTUNE magazine. All rights reserved.)

Other corporations provide their own innovative solutions to these problems. In many cases, communities are endangered by social problems gnawing at their foundations. Businesses are responding by joining forces with the nonprofit sector and government to seek solutions that will restore economic and social stability to cities and neighborhoods. Corporate community service, implemented through volunteer programs in more than 1,200 companies throughout America, is benefiting both the communities and the corporations. Corporate employees and retirees are reaching out to the child-at-risk and the senior citizen; the homeless and the poorly educated; the individual and the family in need. (Reprinted from a paid advertising section prepared for the November 2, 1992 issue of FORTUNE magazine. All rights reserved).

Across the United States many companies are participating in Adopt-a-School programs. In Texas, high-tech firms including Electronic Data Systems, Alcatel Network Systems, Northern Telecom, and Fujitsu Network Transmission Systems partner with the Richardson Independent School District. For example, Alcatel adopted Mark Twain Elementary School and has donated more than 50 Macintosh computers, plus the hardware to link them in a network, according to Mike Newsom, Alcatel's manager of media and public relations.[5] Software giant Microsoft provides Family Technology Nights to introduce parents to educational software. Parents get discounts on Microsoft's software, and the host schools receive donated software from Microsoft.[6] Other corporations are forming partnerships and sponsoring programs to get the latest technology into the classroom.

As a global company Pfizer Inc. seeks to improve living conditions and create economic and educational opportunities for people worldwide. The corporation extends philanthropic support to a range of U.S.-based organizations that address international issues including foreign policy concerns and programs in health, education, and other areas. In addition, through various subsidiaries and affiliates outside the United States, Pfizer provides support to institutions and organizations in many countries and regions throughout the world. For example, in 1992 Pfizer made a three-year $45,000 pledge to Co-operation Ireland, an organization dedicated to building mutual respect and understanding between the people of Northern Ireland and the Republic of Ireland.[7] This program emphasizes youth and student cross-border exchange programs as a road to peace.

"We take our responsibilities to society very seriously," states Johnson & Johnson Chairman and CEO Ralph S. Larsen. "It is a concept which has become ingrained in our corporate culture and strongly influences the way we do business. We would not consider ourselves successful as a corporation if we were to fall short as a good corporate citizen."[8] Providing at-risk youths with the skills needed to enter and remain in the workforce is the objective of

J&J's Bridge to Employment Program. A partnership with the National Alliance of Business, the program calls upon local government, businesses, schools, community groups, and families to work together to assist young people. Bridge to Employment has been introduced to selected towns and cities in Florida, Puerto Rico, New Jersey, and Texas. This program in Playa de Ponce, Puerto Rico, provided counseling as well as training in clerical skills and English at the Sister Isolina Ferre Center for Young People for them who had left school and were unemployed. All found jobs in their community.[9]

HOLISTIC APPROACH

Responsible corporations know that traditional philanthropy alone cannot solve racial tensions and world violence. However, a holistic approach combining resources, talent, leadership, and dollars can significantly contribute to GlobalSolutions in the Transformation Age.

TRANSFORMATIONAL LEADERSHIP

Organizations in the Transformation Age need to focus on the selection and development of transformational leaders. In his article, "How To Lead A Revolution" (*Fortune,* November 28, 1994), Thomas A. Stewart cites several corporate leaders who are successfully leading their divisions or entire companies through major change. Doug Cahill, general manager of Olin Pool Products, created "an organization so flat you could stick it under a door."[10] In this new structure there are only two division job titles, coach and teammate.

Transformational leadership is a prerequisite for the successful corporation of the Transformation Age. Managers can either react to changes in the Transformation Age or they can transform themselves and their companies to meet the demands for speed and global reach. "If you do incremental change," says Jerre Stead, former CEO of AT&T Global Information Solutions (which was NCR before it was acquired), "you'll never get there."[11]

Another transformational leader is Art Zafiropoulo. General Signal had hired Mr. Zafiropoulo primarily for his knowledge of Japan. In 1990 General Signal Corporation asked him to turn around Ultratech, one of their semiconductor divisions. Ultratech was fast losing marketshare. Knowing that Ultratech could not compete directly with Nikon and Canon on their home turf, Mr. Zafiropoulo wisely changed their target customer. The move worked and profit returned in 1991.

Mr. Zafiropoulo's marketing strategy was successful because he was thoroughly overhauling the company's operations at the same time. He boosted morale and launched a quality drive that improved productivity. The company did so well that in 1992 Mr. Zafiropoulo led a management buyout. Renamed Ultratech Stepper Inc., the company's sales jumped 53 percent to $54 million in 1993. Today Ultratech is an independent company that is leading the Japanese in their own market. Revenues should hit $89.7 million for 1994 and are expected to climb.[12] This dramatic transformation is an excellent case study of how to restructure a company while executing a radical shift in the company's marketing strategy.

Robert J. House, a professor at the Wharton School of Management, cites four common characteristics of transformational leaders. These leaders:

- Have a vision of a better future—a future to which the group has a right and of which it can be proud.
- Possess courage of their convictions.
- Place confidence in their followers and confidence in high standards.
- Are driven by the satisfaction of building the organization, seeing people develop, and accomplishing things through others.[13]

TRANSFORMATIONAL LEADERS

The best transformational leaders do not sell their vision—they help others buy it. Their strength lies not in their leadership but in their followers. Transformational leaders encourage each worker as an individual to grasp and live the culture change.

CORPORATE CHOICES

A survey of 778 American and European multinational companies reveals that many are reengineering themselves to compete in the new world economy brought about by collapsing communism, falling trade barriers, and emerging trade blocs such as the North American Free Trade Agreement and the Asia-Pacific Economic Cooperation forum. "The findings of this research indicate colossal change, tantamount to turmoil," reports Louis Harris and Associates in New York City, who conducted the survey for management consulting firm A.T. Kearney Inc.[14] The vast majority of those companies covered in the survey—353 from North America and 425 from Europe—sell in all the major markets.

Nearly two-thirds of the companies reported that their overriding concerns are improving cost-competitiveness and changing their marketing strategies. Also more than half intend to overhaul organizational structures, diversify workforces, and broaden international scope. Plans for global expansion differed sharply by nation. Some 83 percent of Dutch firms intend to expand into global markets, followed by 75 percent of German and French, 72 percent of British, and just 35 percent and 33 percent of Canadian and Spanish firms, respectively.[15]

For current corporations to meet the new demands of doing business as global organizations, more is required than just change. Global companies need to make clear choices that will lead to these transformations:

- **Business as usual companies into GlobalOrganizations** with visionary leaders who create a fluid corporate structure that can respond instantly to changing global needs.

- **Company Vision into GlobalVision** which encourages implementation of innovative strategies to bring products to the global marketplace.

- **Company Culture into GlobalCulture** which synthesizes the diverse cultures of employees at the individual, societal, and organizational level.

- **Company Teams into GlobalWork Teams** which combine complementary skills of employees into integrated teams at the management and workgroup level.

- **Company Problem Solving into GlobalSolutions** which result in corporate international success by continuing the process of organizational transformation.

New terms, such as GlobalVision, GlobalSolutions, and GlobalThink have been created for this book to more effectively describe global issues.

As workplace borders expand and the mobility of the workforce increases, new concepts are needed to manage cross-cultural teams which are fast becoming the basic structure for today's multinational corporation. This transformation raises a serious question, "Can any single corporate culture embrace the new transnational company?" What tools and skills are necessary to educate, train, and motivate employees who survived the downsizings, reorganizations, mergers, buyouts, and expansions into the global marketplace? How can we move out of the collision of cultures and into a tolerant stage of *live and let live*—into a truly cooperative culture?

COLLABORATIVE CULTURE

We must learn new ways of working in our multicultural world. We can stubbornly cling to the old culture we know best or we can together redesign work creating a collaborative workgroup culture.

The starting point for these successful ventures must be mutual cultural respect. Then the process can go forward, as individuals collectively explore new ways of working together to reach company goals. This book will open new perspectives for readers as we highlight how some global companies—though continents apart—tackle the challenges of conducting business successfully in the Transformation Age. The opportunities are out there for those companies who want to blaze new trails in the international arena.

Chapter 2

Is Corporate Culture Dead?

Is Corporate Culture Dead?

Corporate culture can work in the 21st Century—but only if it is transformed. For corporate culture, as companies have developed and communicated that culture for decades, is no longer viable. In *Corporate Cultures: The Rites and Rituals of Corporate Life,* Terence E. Deal and Allen A. Kennedy defined corporate culture as a cohesion of values, myths, heroes, and symbols—"the way we do things around here."[1] They pointed to the early leaders of American business, such as Thomas Watson of IBM, Harley Procter of Procter & Gamble, and General Johnson of Johnson & Johnson, who believed that strong culture brought success. These leaders saw their role as creating an environment in their corporations in which employees could be secure and accomplish the work necessary for business success. They paid almost fanatical attention to the culture of their companies and passed down these lessons from one generation of managers to another. And many executives have continued the process.

GENERAL ELECTRIC'S CORPORATE REVOLUTION

When Jack Welch became Chief Executive Officer of General Electric in 1981, he realized that GE's corporate culture had to be changed. He has relentlessly pursued an agenda of change so radical, so fundamental, and so threatening that it amounts to a revolution. Welch communicated his new message, "Changing the culture starts with an attitude. I hope you won't think I'm being melodramatic if I say that the institution ought to stretch itself, ought to reach, to the point where it almost comes unglued."[2]

When Welch began, GE had nearly 420,000 workers on its payroll. Over the years their ranks increased by acquiring companies and decreased by selling businesses and cutting positions. By July 1993, GE had approximately 230,000 employees.

In *Control Your Destiny or Someone Else Will* by Noel M. Tichy and Stratford Sherman, the methods Welch has used to create this quantum change are described as a three-act drama. Although the three acts usually overlap, each depends on the one before. Act I was the awakening to the need for change and was largely accomplished by late 1985. Completed in 1988, Act II involved the creation of an organizational blueprint for the future. Act III is more complex because it pushes cultural change by moving the company toward the use of targeted teams who have the authority to define solutions to business problems. This 10-year program, which began in 1988, is still being presented on an on-going basis to every employee. Ultimately, Welch wants this program to nurture a new organization free of boundaries with integrated diversity and global leadership.

Because of all this change, Welch defines an effective corporate executive as "someone who can change the tires while the car's still rolling."[3] John Trani, who leads Milwaukee-based General Electric Medical Systems (GEMS), fits that description. GEMS is GE's most complex global enterprise, composed of their U.S. operations in Milwaukee, Yokogawa Medical Systems in Japan, and Thompson-CGR in France. GEMS' globalization required unprecedented levels of teamwork among people who did not know each other, felt they had little in common, and in some cases distrusted each other. This is the type of challenge corporations across the world are experiencing today.

Yes, business in the 1990s has changed—*drastically*—and corporations are struggling to adapt. Companies are now working with former competitors and are seeking to become superconductors of ideas, information, production, and people. The natural convergence between primary culture, work culture, and corporate culture is one of the greatest challenges to domestic companies that are setting up international offices or global partnerships—especially if they try to impose their corporate culture on workers from diverse primary cultures.

GLOBALPOSITIONING

A crossborder buyout race is emerging even though at least half of all crossborder acquisitions by global corporations fail. According to KPMG Peat Marwick, the worldwide volume of crossborder acquisitions was a record $110 billion in 1994—an increase of 64 percent. [4]

A dramatic shift has occurred in corporate America's strategic thinking as U.S. multinationals have taken a predominant role in the global acquisition sweepstakes. This is in contrast to the 1980s' merger-and-acquisition mania when U.S. companies concentrated on domestic deals. Two main reasons explain the involvement of U.S. multinationals of all sizes in acquiring crossborder companies:

- The greatest opportunities for growth are in the international markets—especially in Latin America, Western Europe, Eastern Europe, and parts of Asia.
- Acquisitions are the quickest method of grabbing market position.

"Most mergers fail to deliver on their profit promises, and a new wave of deals may mean more of the same old mistakes," states Anne B. Fisher in "How to Make a Merger Work."[5] When multinationals buy non-U.S. companies, they are taking big risks. The aftermath is that managers and workers from different corporate and national cultures often struggle to adjust to a strange new environment.

CORPORATE CHEMISTRY

Any merger is doomed if there is no real effort beforehand to see whether the two cultures have anything in common. Yet top management too often regards cultural chemistry as a troublesome detail that can be left to the human resource department.

Says Warren Hellman: "Be leery of anybody who tells you to go ahead and do a deal that looks good on paper, with the idea of fixing the 'people problems' later."[6] The hundreds of tiny components that make up a company's personality—everything from styles of dress, to whether employees are on a first-name basis, to the number of meetings that are deemed necessary to get a job done—are not easily altered. Companies with clashing cultures can end up, like a miserable married couple, living as strangers under the same roof.

In a crossborder acquisition, corporate management must move cautiously, even diplomatically. Handling a crossborder buyout requires the new management to nudge, cajole, persuade, and negotiate change with employees from cultures entirely different from their own.

HAWORTH INC.

Management must also not offend the political powers in the local country. Emerging countries will be especially sensitive to this issue because of the need to create jobs. "You can't push it," says Gerald Johanneson, president of Haworth Inc. of Holland, Michigan. "You have to let the employees pull you."[7]

Over the past six years, Haworth has acquired six European companies. With an estimated $191 million in 1994 sales, the company is now considered one of the largest furniture makers in Europe. Because of the company's lack of international experience, it is learning firsthand how it should merge European and U.S. cultures.

The diversity of Europe's markets is a challenge to Haworth to integrate and swap the six companies' product technology, distribution channels, research and development, parts and talent. Additionally, the company must get optimal results from differing information technologies, procurement systems, and manufacturing.

At an early stage, Haworth committed to giving European managers the responsibility to integrate and direct the acquisitions. Manfred H. von Prondzinski, who speaks four languages, leads the group as vice president of European operations. Eleven other managers are located in Paris and at the company's headquarters in Holland, Michigan.

A radical cultural change will be necessary for Haworth's subsidiaries to cooperate fully with one another. According to Mr. von Prondzinski, the subsidiaries will have to shed competitive instincts—their "us against them" attitude—and understand the benefits each will have through cooperation.[8]

Three years ago French managers at Mobilier International, Haworth furniture subsidiary in Paris, resisted purchasing products from a sister company in Portugal, Cortal & Seldex. Today that mindset has changed. Haworth has emphasized the need to leverage the unique products and national distribution channels of each of the companies. By the end of the decade, the company wants to more than double European sales to $470 million—a pace approximately twice as fast as the projected growth of the European market. To achieve this goal, cooperation between the two companies is essential.

Haworth has found that any time a change affecting workers is needed, the company is faced with inflexible industry contracts and restrictive national labor laws. Referring to local human resource officers and their books filled with government regulations,

A. Randall Evans, the company's human resources manager, says, "They are keepers of rules. If you're trying to be a change agent, there's a lot of resistance around government regulations."[9]

RHONE-POULENE

Some experts say Rhone-Poulene SA, the diversified French chemical maker, made too many deals too fast. The U.S. operations for Rhone-Poulene are still struggling to make its acquisitions work—and this is nine years after the company's first purchase. The challenge has been to streamline and harmonize the operations of 18 companies:

- 250 different pension and compensation plans.
- More than 100 largely incompatible software packages.
- Corporate cultures from small entrepreneurial businesses to divisions. of big U.S. companies that have been cast off.[10]

John A. Wichtrich, an executive vice president at the U.S. operations, admits that "There was an underestimation of the importance of cultural integration."[11] According to a company adviser, "Rhone-Poulene studied the financials, but the people were ignored." He feels conditions have worsened considerably after the years of upheaval. "The employees are shell-shocked. You've got a real crisis on your hands," argues this adviser.[12]

The creation of a new matrix management structure has called for U.S. and French managers to share power over key decisions. This has only increased employees' confusion. CEO Peter J. Neff says, "It's difficult to pull people together if they are being pulled in different directions."[13]

Resolution of the problems that have plagued the U.S. operations is expected to be achieved by the latest reorganization. U.S. managers have set up an umbrella sales organization to address customer needs. As a result, customers will be able to buy most of their products through a single sales contract and then be billed electronically.

It has been a long time since chief executives have been as eager to make merger deals as they are right now. As with the great merger booms of the 1960s and the mid-1980s, this one, too, will leave its mark on shareholder returns, business strategies, and corporate cultures. As companies continue their look to the future and to the partners who can give them GlobalPosition, mergers are themselves becoming a powerful agent of further transformations that will redefine the nature of markets and competition. One of the most intense contests for future positioning is in the information-highway arena. For example, in order to gain the most powerful position in this field, companies in computers (hardware and software), telecommunications, television, and multimedia production are merging, acquiring, and forming new alliances at such an accelerated speed that Federal Trade Commission regulations and legal implications cannot keep pace.

So how can a fictitious conglomerate composed of such players as Microsoft, Fox Cable, AT&T, Disney, and CBS form any kind of *single* corporate culture? The speed with which alliances and mergers are made raises the question of whether any single corporate culture can work for today's transnational corporations.

And what does this mean for such global corporations? Should they abort the teamwork concept? Do they throw up their hands and say they cannot develop a corporate culture? Or can their workforces learn the dynamics of working globally—crossing cultures, job functions, and industries?

THERMO ELECTRON CORPORATION

From its base in Waltham, Massachusetts, Thermo Electron Corporation faces these challenges but has always looked to the wider world. Founder and chief executive George N. Hatsopoulos was born in Greece, emigrated to the United States and, upon graduation from MIT in 1956, founded the company. Thermo now generates nearly 40 percent of its $1.6 billion in annual sales from international locations, and 35 percent of its shareholders live abroad.[14]

This broad global exposure gives Thermo Electron more expertise—and more leverage in international markets—than most American companies its size. And Mr. Hatsopoulos hopes that international sales increase to 50 percent by the year 2000. This science-based conglomerate's global sales are now concentrated in Western Europe, but they plan to expand into three very difficult markets: China, Russia, and India.

What may give Thermo a distinct edge multinationally is its unusual structure and composition. The company produces and sells an enormous range of products worldwide. Their equipment powers environment-friendly buses in Brazil, monitors air quality in Egypt and Japan, tests Dutch computers against lightning strikes, monitors the radioactivity in European nuclear-powered plants, and checks the quality of beverage bottles in Argentina. Companies from outside the United States also buy Thermo's power plants, paper recycling equipment, heart pumps, and mammography systems.

And the product list keeps growing, mainly because Mr. Hatsopoulos is that rare mix of scientist and successful entrepreneur who understands cultural differences. He has attracted creative people with good technical skills and has rewarded them well for their performance. So it is no surprise that he has piloted his company to consistent growth. In 1983, looking for investment capital to diversify his business, he spun off a subsidiary named Thermedics. He has since sold off nine other businesses, always keeping a majority share for himself. The Hatsopoulos approach gives subsidiary CEOs considerable autonomy and resources.

The company's culture provides a broad framework offering incentives and fostering an environment for employees to create new ideas and products. "That strategy gives Thermo the heft of a 300-pound lineman but the agility of a cornerback."[15] This combination permits subsidiaries to develop the strategy that suits them best when tackling international markets. Some subsidiaries find it more advantageous to manufacture product in the United States and capture other markets via exports, while others manufacture abroad for national or regional markets. Thermo's global reach and global strategy—to spot emerging demands early and come up with an appropriate product—positions the corporation as a leading global player for the 21st Century. The company has created vision shared by its teams or subsidiaries and is allowing these teams to create their own processes for working as units.

CORPORATE CULTURE

First, the transnational corporation must create a vision of the company and its direction. This vision becomes the basis of the new corporate culture.

CORPORATE VISION

The act of creating a corporate vision—visioning—is a time of collective reflection and futuring. The future comes each second— ready or not. "We fear it, hope for it, push it, note it on desk calendars, but far too few of us have learned to love it—to create it thoughtfully and imaginatively," says Stephen Silha in *Creative Living*. "In one sense, there is no future, because the future is now," he continues. "That's why futurists talk about *alternative futures*. Many different possible futures can happen simultaneously." Silha points out that futurist Robert Theobald states that in our constantly changing world, "Humans don't function well if they don't have time for reflection . . . We need time to find our center, to get away from our sense of overload. New ideas and solutions come when you get rested."[16]

Visioning is an emotional process. "It looks at possibilities; it imagines what could be; it creates excitement. For a vision to take hold, it must tap into people's aspirations and their intuitive sense of the future. The vision needs to be seen as a breakthrough so that people are willing to challenge their own beliefs," says W. Mathew Juechter, CEO of ARC International, Ltd.[17]   Visioning creates a sense of purpose and presents a shared picture of the organization's future.

Vision is not just a set of words. Vision is a feeling about a place where people want to go, and about a way to get there. Until a company creates a process that allows people to sense how things will be different, there will be no vision. In *Competing for the Future*, authors Gary Hamel and C. K. Prahalad point out that developing vision requires encouraging dialogue across functional and geographic divisions.[18]   Instead of mapping out strategy to preserve existing marketshare, managers must look for *opportunity share* to determine possible future markets, technologies, and customers perhaps not now in existence. As part of their vision, managers must assess in what new markets corporate competencies might be profitable.

EXAMPLES OF GLOBAL VISION

Motorola envisions a world in which people, not places, will have phone numbers; where hand-held devices will link people anywhere; and where such devices can deliver text and video along with sound.[19]   To create this world, Motorola realizes it will need to strengthen competencies in digital compression, flat-screen displays, and battery technology. It also will have to increase the recognition of its brand in the minds of global consumers. Motorola's vision includes—like all corporate visions should— foresight. Hamel and Prahalad point out that foresight is based on deep insights into technology trends, demographics, regulations, and lifestyle, and how these can be harnessed to rewrite the rules and create new competitive space.[20]   Firms that create the future are unorthodox and rule-breaking subversives. As much as anything, their vision and foresight comes from the desire to make a real difference in people's lives.

Sony Director Akio Morita says, "Our plan is to lead the public with new products rather than ask them what kind of products they want. The public does not know what is possible, but we do."[21] Trying to give customers what they want often means copying innovators. The goal isn't to benchmark competitors but to outpace them. Corporations that create the future do more than just satisfy customers. They constantly amaze them. Corporate vision should include this type of foresight.

These visionary leaders are constantly working to create tomorrow. Another visionary example began in 1906 when a young Russian immigrant found work as an office boy at Marconi Wireless Telegraph Company. He worked his way up to chief inspector at the age of 22. And ever watchful for ways to advance in his career, he decided to attend a demonstration of a new kind of circuit—one that could generate continuous electromagnetic waves. The young man returned to work, convinced he had seen the future. Memos flew. He described how music could be broadcast to thousands of homes at once, and from a single transmitter. Every family in America would buy a *radio box*. And Marconi would manufacture and sell every one. The company's more senior managers thought he had lost his mind. Besides, they were in the telegraph business. But later, Marconi Wireless became the Radio Corporation of America (RCA).[22] And a visionary leader—the former office boy, David Sarnoff—became its president.

Other company examples of vision with foresight are JVC's desire to give programming control back to TV viewers, Apple's vision to make computers friendly, and CNN's dream to provide news around-the-clock for a global society that no longer works only in America.

GLOBALVISION

Once the corporate vision is created, it should be communicated and adapted worldwide. One of the most effective communication methods is to depict it graphically.

COMMUNICATING THE VISION

National Semiconductor, based in Santa Clara, California, used a graphic design to promote global integration and an understanding of its vision that can be viewed by all employees. Hanging a graphic vision (3 feet by 14 feet) on the wall and inviting discussion encourages the local interpretations that bring it to life. It can be communicated easily through various media and combined with interactive workshops and communication sessions. Large graphic images seem less formal than written documents and are not as readily associated with multicultural biases. If a vision evolves with feedback from local sites, it can eventually display enough elements that a wide range of people can see their relationship to it—literally seeing themselves working together.

This process of participating in the vision increases awareness that cross-cultural strategic alliances and joint ventures are good for the company. People need to see and understand the concept's relevance to their own personal roles and responsibilities. Only then will they be capable of overcoming the discomfort of multicultural work environments. As more and more organizations become network-based, distributed, and multicultural, these integrating frameworks will become essential tools for communication—as in the case of National Semiconductor Corporation.

NATIONAL SEMICONDUCTOR

With 28,000 employees in operations across the world, a team of corporate staff members worked to define a new vision with the top 500 managers and to communicate it to all employees. David Sibbet of Grove Consultants International created the graphic visioning process at National. "This is the first company I know of that has a GUI (graphic user interface) on its overall strategic process," Sibbet states.[23] The visions were used to provide a larger context for redesign efforts, backdrops for communication sessions, and management team building.

However, this graphic approach was not universally accepted by employees. A completely customized design was needed for Asia, making sure the supervisors played a key role. Scotland, with its independent culture, needed direct involvement in the design process. The lessons learned from Semiconductor's global visioning were:

- The process of creating visions is just as important as the vision itself.
- Agreeing on visions and values creates bonds between senior managers that can help them withstand the inherent volatility of plans in an innovative business environment. The secret is keeping the process visible, explicit, and accessible.
- A corporate vision can stimulate related visions from different business units.
- The use of key words and simple graphics allows for understanding by many cultures.
- The vision should be a living communication which means it should reflect new ideas and changing views of the environment. Its framework must be open enough to accept a diversity of interpretations while maintaining its overall integrity.
- Top management's participation in the creation of and commitment to the vision—in the behavior they model—is critical.[24]

Translating Vision into Corporate Culture

Once the company vision is created, the development of the corporate culture begins. The transnational corporation can become a new entity with a dynamic strategic corporate culture, defining that culture in such a way as to get buy-in from its international workforce. This transformation can be accomplished by training corporate managers and employees to understand the new culture and motivating them to champion it.

CORPORATE CULTURE

The solution lies not in spending years of negotiation to form a corporate value system but in creating an umbrella corporate vision—one that is easily communicated. Within the framework of this corporate culture each project team can develop its own dynamic culture.

An appropriate term for this type of team culture is *kinetic*. The word, kinetic, comes from a branch of science (kinetics) that deals with the effects of forces upon the motions of material bodies or with the changes in a physical or chemical system. Thus a kinetic process culture is formed by a team of individuals from diverse cultures who, through the forces of their cultures, develop a work system to successfully complete their projects.

Corporate culture should function much like Houston's Mission Control works for NASA launches. The staff of Mission Control headquarters at Johnson Space Center shares its vision for each mission with the flight crew. President John F. Kennedy in 1961 aptly described the vision of the NASA moon mission as "Achieving the goal, before this decade is out, of landing a man on the moon and returning him safely to earth."[25] The center provides knowledge, training, product (the capsule and booster rockets), fuel, technology expertise, and a project map for the flight. B countdown, they test for corrections in operating procedu. check the astronauts for their readiness and ability to perforn tasks. In preparation for the launch and at all points during the mission, control staff take readings of weather conditions and the changing environment. They make recommendations on flaws and challenges which occur during orbit. Although they maintain some control over the mission, they provide discretionary control to the crew and allow this team to operate the on-board experiments and to manually maneuver the space craft. The flight truly becomes a joint effort between Mission Control, its satellites, and the space crew.

In the same way, corporate culture provides a framework for getting things done and distinguishes one company's efforts from another. "Culture establishes a unique set of formal and informal ground rules for how we think, how we behave, and what we assume to be true," explains Daryl R. Conner in *Managing at the Speed of Change*.[26] A transnational corporation is actually an aggregate of subcultures—individual teams around the world—and their collective viewpoint or vision serves as a corporate common bond. However, the individual teams must, in turn, create their own culture or process for working as team units. Their vision is shared and provides a cohesiveness among employees throughout the organization and at the individual team level. The culture—at both corporate and team levels—must be dynamic to allow for changing players, alliances, and the diversity of projects. Unless a corporate culture calls for broad companywide goals and the structuring of kinetic team process cultures, employees will continue to operate within their own values and beliefs, creating cultural barriers to globalization.

As companies rapidly move toward implementing the teamwork approach, structuring a process for each project's GlobalWork team culture becomes an imperative. And a global corporate vision—a shared view of broad goals and directions—must substitute for the more complex glue of an extensive, rigid corporate culture.

Corporate culture must be fluid, open, collaborative, relaxed, and "expectant." Corporate culture is the shell that protects the egg—the mother's physical environment that nurtures the embryo and brings a baby to life. In *Leadership and the New Science,* Margaret Wheatley argues that the organization should be seen as a living system. If you "switch your metaphor to one of dynamic processes—which is what happens when you think of organizations as living systems," then corporate culture becomes an environment you create to sustain life, she contends.[27] Mathew Juechter agrees. He sees the organization as a series of circles that overlap where people come together naturally to accomplish work. These circles flow and interact with one another in the same way that living cells do.[28] More specific cultural guidelines are best defined at the team level. These guidelines may include such aspects as dress code, facility design, management philosophy, ethics, business development, selection and development of employees, reward systems, benefits, and focus of work.

CORPORATE CULTURE AND REWARD SYSTEMS

"By changing their cultures without also developing a reward system, companies run the risk of sending employees terribly mixed signals and are much less likely to sustain any gains," on the other hand, simply changing the reward system in the hope that the reward system can fix the company's cultural problems, companies often end up throwing money at their problems, says Elizabeth J. Hawk.[29] Yet, while the key to flexible organization is often increased teamwork, the team concept is neither a *silver bullet* nor an *easy fix*. It isn't enough to gather a group of people sprinkle some magic dust on them, and say, "Poff, you're a team." Developing effective teams takes much more than magic dust.[30] When a company sets up a team, it should be prepared to provide ongoing training and communication—as well as team-based reward—to back up the change effort.

Although corporations still need individual contributions in some situations, most company's work is conducted through teamwork. Now, more than ever, employees must be able to work together to achieve the complex goals most corporations require.

Skill or competency based pay design, for example, requires that the organization discover which competencies are necessary for its success, then brings that analysis down to the team or individual level and rewards employees for acquiring those skills. Therefore, the company swifts, from paying for the job to paying the team member for what they bring to the job.

"When you reward for results, there's more at work then just pay," Hawk continues. "But sooner or later, employees will begin to ask, 'What's in it for me?' That's why a new way of getting work done must be supported by a new approach to rewards."[31]

James C. Collins and Jerry I. Porras, authors of *Built To Last,* provide insight into the core ideologies companies include in their corporate vision and culture. They cite these companies for their corporate cultures and successful core ideologies.

Wal-Mart:	To provide value to customers, to buck conventional wisdom, to work with passion and commitment, to run lean, and to pursue ever-higher goals.
Nordstrom:	Service to the customer above all else, hard work and productivity, continuous improvement, excellence in reputation, and being part of something special.
Procter & Gamble:	Product excellence, continuous self-improvement, honesty, and respect and concern for the individual.
Merck:	We try never to forget that medicine is for people. It's not for the profits. The profits follow . . . (George Merck)[32]

ADAPTIVE CULTURES

Corporations that create fluid, adaptive cultures with visions supported by core ideologies allow for a blending of teams of different but unique combinations of skills and technologies to meet the requirements of individual customers. These companies are then able to listen and adapt to customers and to outperform nonadaptive companies in terms of net income growth and return on investment. This type of corporation calls for a kind of flexibility that most of us have not even imagined yet.

For those corporations willing to make the commitment to create the future with GlobalVision and to meet the challenges of multicultural teamwork, the rewards—and satisfactions—can be great. As Will Rogers said, "Even if you're on the right track, you'll get run over if you just sit there."[33]

Chapter 3

The Impact of Culture on Teamwork

The Impact of Culture on Teamwork

The concept of achieving corporate goals through teamwork has been the management style of the 90s. However, in recent months, research has found that all is not well in traditional *teamland.* Corporate leaders are witnessing that interpersonal dynamics have as much impact, both positive and negative, on the effectiveness of a team as do their technical skills. They are recognizing that teamwork is a process that must constantly be assessed and restructured to help teams achieve their goals efficiently and effectively. However, this process has proven to be more difficult than companies had at first imagined, even when team members are from the same country. When transnational companies attempt to form teams with members from diverse cultures, the process becomes infinitely more complex.

As the goals and configurations of teams change in response to the demands of the global market, teams are increasingly required to cross boundaries at all levels of the organization (e.g., cross-functional, cross-location, cross-cultural). Corporate leaders are finding it increasingly difficult to organize and lead teams to work together to deliver products and services to meet the changing needs of the global consumer.

Teams struggle with the transition from a focus on individual achievement to a focus on shared goals and teamwork. One reason for this problem may stem from use of the word *team* itself. Because of today's sports team image, team players in football, soccer, basketball, polo, baseball, or hockey focus on what it takes to win the game. Their motivation stems from the competitive desire to win and the fame and money that follow. For years corporate teams have operated with similar goals. This approach is no longer effective.

TEAM SUCCESS

Workgroup success depends on cultivating an entirely new mindset. If the main team focus is to outperform other groups within the company or in other competitive companies, the team process will not produce the desired results.

Rather, decisions must be made concerning the competencies that existing employees or teams bring or do not bring to the process. If specific competencies are needed to achieve goals, corporations may need to hire additional people or sometimes go outside the company to work collaboratively with work teams provided by other corporations.

Training magazine's October 1994 industry report reveals that national enthusiasm for organizing employees into teams seems to have waned over the past two years. In 1992, 82 percent of all organizations participating in the survey identified some of their workgroups as teams. The figure in 1994 is 73 percent. Two years ago, 35 percent of all U.S. organizations revealed that some of their teams were self-directed or self-managed. Only 28 percent made that claim in 1994.[1]

Most recent books addressing the team concept are focusing on two types: self-directed and cross-functional. Data on self-directed work teams centers mainly on empowerment and highlights the negative impact of these teams. Ed Lawler, director of the Center for Effective Organizations at the University of Southern California, calls these teams the *Mercedes of the workforce* because of their high cost of maintenance.

Cross-functional teams have evolved from the total quality management (TQM) movement, and their purpose is to bring together individuals from different corporate departments (i.e., manufacturing, marketing, customer service, and sales) to work on a specific product. This concept mainly emphasizes an understanding of each job function and how the variety of views can improve the product and process from design to market introduction.

Teams composed of members from the same country and similar cultures often have difficulty working together effectively. The challenges faced by international corporations with transnational team members bring new complexities. These companies must seek GlobalSolutions—innovative approaches to creating and managing not just teams but also the impact of cultural diversity on team process.

Once individual team members have explored the wide definition of culture and identified their own values and how they differ from other cultures, they realize that all behavior in everyday life and business is culturally oriented. This realization becomes a tool for comprehending why behavior perceived as normal within other cultures may look abnormal to them. Team members behave in a way that is normal to them because that is the way they grew up, and their set of behaviors are those for which they have been rewarded. However, for people of one culture to communicate and manage people from other cultures, they must first understand how their own values may conflict with the values of different cultures.

THE LANGUAGE FACTOR

One of the most apparent differences in diverse workgroups is language. In a global society, studying languages should be a major emphasis for U.S. school systems since America is far behind other countries in language education. Corporations are realizing the need to expand the language competencies of their workforce. They often provide language courses and English-as-a-second-language (ESL) training and reward employees for their achievements. Companies are finding that most employees are more creative and productive in their native language. Consequently, forcing them to continually use a second language at work can deprive the company of their best work performance.

Most companies select an official corporate language that becomes the principal conduit of corporate communications. They should have explicit language policies for sales and customer service representatives and for all international business environments. Management should also consider translation of major communiqués in other languages as crucial to corporate-wide understanding and collaboration. Translating newsletters, annual reports, and other publications into the primary languages of employees, stockholders, and customers facilitates the communication process and emphasizes the importance of each of these individuals to the company. Whenever possible, graphics and diagrams with accompanying translations should be used for more effective communication across cultures.

Molex, with 70 percent of sales overseas and 42 offices in 19 countries, prides itself on being a very global company and wants that to be self-evident in its annual report. They do not feel it is necessary to translate the entire report, but they translate the annual summary into other languages. Molex picked Japanese because a third of its business is in Japan; German and French because they are the primary European languages (its headquarters is also in Germany); and Mandarin because it does almost 18 percent of its business in the southern countries of the Far East, where the language is commonly spoken.[2] Trinova Corporation also translates its report for the highly attractive Chinese market. "A lot less people speak English there, so you do need a companion piece (in Mandarin)," points out Richard Rump, manager of financial communications for Trinova Corp., a $1.6 billion Maumee, Ohio, maker of such products as valves, hoses, motors, and generators.[3]

English is the mother tongue of 300-450 million people and is spoken with varying degrees of facility by up to one-third of the world's population. Although English is referred to as the universal language and is taught in most countries across the world, cross-cultural communication is far more than the literal translation of words. Nor does an exchange of words mean that everyone shares the same meanings and assumptions.

GLOBAL COMMUNICATION

Global communication requires the ability to translate the cultural meaning behind the words and to anticipate the impact of spoken or written words in another culture. Even the translation of silence is important to intercultural understanding.

GlobalWork teams should also select an official team language, which may or may not be the official corporate language. They need to discover ways of defining meanings, as well as using visual symbols to clarify communication. Some companies have developed on-line dictionaries for team members—especially those who work in distant locations. Team members who do not speak a second language should learn as many words as possible in the languages spoken by their teammates.

Niklaus Leuenberger, general manager of the Peninsula Hotel in New York City, understands language challenges and cites this example: "In establishing a hotel dedicated to meeting international standards, one always has to take local cultures into account."[4] When he helped open the first Western-managed hotel in the People's Republic of China in 1981, a problem emerged around the use of Chinese names that could be difficult for Western guests to pronounce. The Chinese managers wanted to give hotel employees identification tags bearing numbers rather than names. Believing numbers would be too impersonal, others suggested they assign English first names for use on the identification tags. A simple solution? Not really. Upset by the prospect of having to use English names, the Chinese demanded that they be allowed to use their full Chinese names or, as a second choice, identification numbers. After weeks of negotiations—focused on getting to know and respect individual and national values—a compromise was reached: each name tag would show an English first name and the Chinese family name. Thus the hotel met its business goal—providing excellent service for guests—and the employees retained their sense of dignity and cultural identity.

CULTURES AND SUBCULTURES

Within each culture there are many subcultures of which an individual is simultaneously a member. Each team member represents a specific subset of cultural values, for example: a German, supervisor, mechanical engineer, and craftsman. A Nigerian electrical engineer, for instance, may have professional values that are strikingly similar to those of a Brazilian counterpart. The extraordinary strength of professional cultures means that they often have more meaning for team members than a corporate culture. And why not? A professional culture is often a lifelong choice—whereas an individual team member can move in and out of a corporate or team culture on a daily basis, literally leaving it at the work site.[5] To transform teams into GlobalWork Teams, managers must first recognize that cultural differences exist and that they must challenge team cooperation at several simultaneous levels.

– *Individual level*

Each individual's cultural perspective is unique. It is the result of a synthesis of cultural influences in different areas of that individual's life (e.g., family, religion, education, profession, company, country).

– *Team level*

When individuals of different cultures join efforts to accomplish common goals, potential cultural conflicts exist, even if the team members are from the same country. The focus of each team is to create an environment, a kinetic workgroup culture, that enables individuals to contribute to the team process and achieve team goals.

– *Organizational level*

To meet the demands of the Transformation Age, global corporations will need teams at every level of the organization—from the executive suite to the production floor. Initially, each of these teams will be challenged to develop a new culture to accomplish their team's goals. Then each team will meet new cultural challenges as they interface with other teams. These teams may be configured:

- Within the organization or with other companies
- Within functions (e.g., within marketing) or across functions (interface of production teams with marketing teams)
- In the same or different countries

CULTURAL UNDERSTANDING

Once cross-cultural workgroups are formed, corporations will need to invest time and resources to bring the team members to *some level of understanding* of the cultural perspectives of other members so they can work together effectively. The level of understanding required is determined by the purpose, goals, and configuration of the team.

For example, a leadership team formed to develop implementation strategies will have a high level of interaction among its members. The members will require a great deal of cultural understanding to achieve team goals. For this type of team, members need to understand their own culture and values and how they are similar to or different from others within their primary culture. This includes such cultural variables as the concepts of time, change, responsibility, participation, communication, and relationships. With a knowledge of their own culture, members should then gain some understanding of the culture and values of other team members. However, team members must be able to negotiate and make compromises to achieve common goals without having to sacrifice their own cultural values. At another level of the organization, members of a construction team may not need a high level of cultural understanding. They may only need a flexible leader who has the ability to work with diverse cultures and a translator who can provide operational instructions for effective team functioning.

Competencies of team members that are essential and are identified at the beginning of a project will change as corporate projects evolve, especially if projects take several years to complete. As different competencies are needed, teams members may be moved to other teams to meet new requirements, and each team's culture will again adapt and reform. In other words, teams will face never-ending transformation and will need to remain as fluid and boundaryless as the corporate vision.

A review of corporate cultures of Apple Computer, Matsushita, Mitsubishi, and Sony illustrate how their corporate cultures often reflect the company's cultural values. Teams throughout each organization can use these corporate values as priorities in the development of their team cultures.

APPLE COMPUTER

Apple Computer, a U.S.-based company with an entrepreneurial corporate culture, promotes a commonly shared value system within the ranks of its employees and subsidiaries worldwide. Apple management has circulated within the company what is known internally as "Apple Values."[6] These corporate values include: empathy for customers, achievement, aggressiveness, positive social contribution, innovative vision, individual performance with the accompanying reward, team spirit, quality, and excellence. As an entrepreneurial company, Apple's management policy is to encourage innovation and vision, quality and excellence, team spirit and good management.

MATSUSHITA, MITSUBISHI, AND SONY

Japanese company cultures are a reflection of the culture of the country, and individuals within each organization must agree upon specific group norms for business survival. If a joint venture is planned with a U.S. corporation, for example, the American company should determine how the Japanese company's values match their own. Many alliances are formed because of mutual interests in technology or market entry. However, many of them fail because of conflict between value systems that cannot be changed or easily adapted.

Even corporate cultures within several Japanese companies point to different values. According to a study by Farid Elashmawi, Matsushita corporate values are policy orientation, customer satisfaction, contribution to society, coexistence, and co-prosperity.[7] On the other hand, Mitsubishi's corporate values include fair play in business, employee orientation, high morale, concern for individuals, and low risk taking.

The values of these two Japanese companies strongly reflect Japanese cultural concepts such as the emphasis on group harmony, long-term relationships, quality, customer service, and contribution to society.

By contrast, the values selected by Sony employees—liberalism, internationalism, positive attitude toward change, "me"-ism, risk-taking, challenges, and zealousness—clearly place Sony more in the line of an entrepreneurial culture with a focus on liberalism, risk-taking, and internationalism.[8] These corporate values are more characteristic of individualistic cultures and may explain why Sony has been so successful in the United States and in other global markets. Sony has obviously been able to adjust their culture to increase the company's ability to succeed worldwide. These values have enabled them to undertake successful joint ventures with many U.S. corporations. In fact, Sony would probably be more successful in an alliance with U.S. companies than with the other two Japanese companies.

AOC MANAGEMENT GROUP

[This company name and several of the nationalities have been altered to protect the proprietary nature of this project.] AOC Management Group is an Australian-based construction management company working on projects with the Egyptian government in the construction of roads, bridges, canals, and water purification systems. It serves as a transnational model for developing effective workgroups at all organizational levels within and across several cultures. To accomplish the goals of this 12-year project, more than 6,000 workers on the construction projects were brought in from Norway, Finland, Great Britain, and India. A variety of management and construction teams were formed to work with the Egyptians.

The Egyptian government is upgrading the skills of its workforce while providing new development programs for various civil projects over a 12-year period. As the facilities are built, Egyptian workers are taught how to maintain and operate the numerous facilities. As a result, every three years a trained group of Egyptians assume the operation of completed facilities.

Although they had sufficient money to fund the project, the Egyptian government soon recognized that this project required an immense amount of expertise and manpower and that Egypt could not supply enough skilled personnel to accomplish these goals in a 12-year time frame. They looked to the global workplace to find the expertise, manpower, and a GlobalSolution.

Obviously, finding a GlobalSolution presented many challenges to the Egyptian leaders. Could they find a company that could supply the wide range of expertise needed—from engineering to training? Could they find enough workers willing to relocate in order to work on this project? How long would they be willing to stay and would they want to bring their families? Where would all the workers live at each site? How would these workers be able to bridge the language barriers at all levels of the project, especially in training the Egyptian workers? These concerns were only the beginning of their challenge.

The Egyptian government contracted with an Australian construction company to help them complete the business development plan and to supply appropriate expertise and personnel to build the facilities and train the Egyptian personnel. Once the project was defined by management teams from Egypt and Australia, the construction company was faced with as many challenges as the Egyptians. Where could they find sufficient personnel with the required skills who would be willing to work on the project? Australia, also, sought a GlobalSolution.

The construction company from Australia contracted with a Norwegian firm to provide engineers for the project. Construction workers were then brought in from Australia, Egypt, Finland, Norway, and Great Britain and equipment operators from India. Now that the company had identified personnel, how would they organize their resources into effective teams to get the work done? How difficult would it be to manage the diverse cultures that would be brought together for this project?

The Australian firm organized teams at all levels of the organization, including on-site teams at project locations around Egypt. Most teams are working together to complete the construction projects. As projects are completed, Norwegian teams will train the Egyptian workers to maintain and operate the completed facilities. This process will then repeat every three years until the project is finished.

Initial formation of workgroup teams from several countries revealed many areas of differences and possible conflict among new team members. Management had to take early proactive steps to bring the teams together to ensure effective communication. Language is one of the many challenges to *getting things done.* While English is the official work language, employees from various countries use their own language with workers from their own culture. Another challenge is the impact of religious issues on the team work schedule. One of the teams is composed of Norwegian workers training Egyptian workers to operate and maintain completed facilities. The two cultures differ in many ways. Norwegian workers prefer to work Monday through Friday with no overtime. They are very task-oriented and accomplish a great deal during the work day. On the other hand, Egyptian workers will only work Monday, Tuesday, Wednesday, Saturday, and Sunday. They do not work on Thursdays and Fridays because these are religious days for them. The length of their day and breaks during the day are also determined by their religious rituals. Since the Australian management team goals required interaction of all groups rather than allowing parallel processes, how did they bring opposite philosophies together so that these teams could accomplish their goals?

First, they realized they could not impose a specific structure on the team. They had to allow the team the freedom to bend their own rules to find a solution. For example, to resolve the differences in work days, the Egyptian and Norwegian team members could work together on Monday, Tuesday, and Wednesday on a dual, overlapping shift. This increased the contact time between the two cultures and accomplished a 10-day work week.

This same flexibility must be used to address every issue that faces the team. Team leaders must be careful not to impose requirements that will cause conflict based on the team's individual differences. Some social separation is natural and should not be prohibited. Productive transnational team relationships require each member to embark on an individual learning journey that most often can be more frustrating than rewarding. However, conducting business across cultures and borders is a requirement for today's global workplace.

The Synthesis of Cultures

The Synthesis of Cultures

The clash of colliding cultures is echoing through city streets and the corridors of corporations, across national borders and the information highways of cyberspace. As corporations merge and form alliances with companies from different geographic areas, the primary challenge is to learn how to get work done with people from diverse cultures. Conflicting cultural values increase the risk of creating misunderstanding, lowering the morale of employees, and often alienating strategic global customers or business partners. Companies are viewing today's world with the same apprehension the Oak Ridge Laboratory scientists years ago must have felt as they worked on the atomic bomb. As they experimented with individual atoms and their combinations, they realized the possibilities of this source of vast potential energy. This atom bomb brought World War II to an end — at the expense of great devastation and loss of life.

In the decades that have followed, scientists have continued to explore the ways to harness this atomic energy—energy that can be liberated by changes in the nucleus of an atom. And they have gone on to discover such positive uses as nuclear power plants. Today companies have the opportunity to find peaceful and creative solutions by learning how to transform the collision of cultures in their intercultural workforce. By first recognizing the challenge and the issues involved, transnational corporations can then harness this energy and reap the rewards of diversity.

Just as the corporate culture creates the environment for all employees to become part of the corporate vision, the kinetic team process culture becomes the environment for the team. The corporate culture must be flexible and broad to allow for alliances, mergers, and acquisitions. The GlobalWork team also must be fluid enough to allow for new cultural mixes as team members from diverse cultures are added or deleted from the group. Change of projects may occur within the same team or, more likely, the team mix will change as the projects change.

FIGURE 4-1

The Synthesis Of Cultures
For GlobalWork Teams

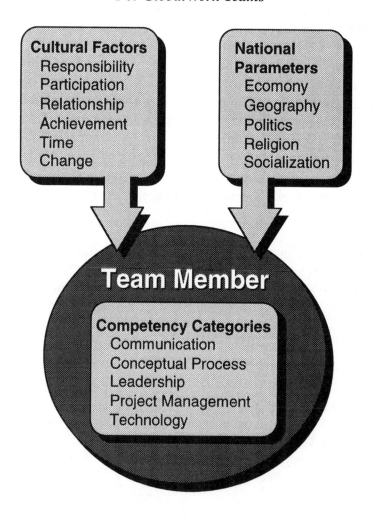

TRANSLATING CULTURE TO CULTURE

The effective transnational team must first have a thorough understanding of the six cultural factors that drive actions taken by individuals within a given nation's parameters of living and governing. In addition to looking inward to each team member's cultural concepts, another important aspect is to look outward to the local specific national parameters of the country where the team is located. National parameters such as politics, religion, socialization, the economy, and geography affect the team's work process. For example, the makeup of the nation is a country parameter that impacts working globally. Such issues as country size, location, and population density often determine the country's ability to import or export in international trade. Location also affects the country's alliances with other nations such as NAFTA and the European Union and is essential for doing business.

Population density also has an impact on the country's use of space. If space is scare, cities such as Tokyo and New York place a high premium on it. In most countries populations are not evenly distributed, for urban areas are usually densely populated while population outside the cities is sparse. Population density also can be a major factor in the location of a corporation's branch office or manufacturing site. National parameters such as these, then, become the operational orientation and values that would permit the company team to function successfully in a given country (see Figure 4-1). Each of these national parameters must be carefully reviewed and analyzed to form an environment in which the team can function. Understanding the influence of each parameter in light of the past, present, and future can facilitate the effectiveness and success of the team.

The competency categories and individual competencies of the team members will be discussed in Chapter 5. This chapter will discuss cultural factors and national parameters of multicultural teams.

CULTURAL FACTORS

Many cultural factors also distinguish one individual from another. The important focus for effective teamwork is for each individual to translate culture to culture—to look carefully at each of the cultures and values—of their own and other team members and understand their meaning. Then a synthesis of cultures can evolve that will allow the team to perform its work effectively.

Rushworth Kidder of the Institute for Global Ethics conducted a global values survey and discovered many common cultural values from his interviews. His list of shared values include love, truth, freedom, fairness, community, tolerance, responsibility, and reverence for life. However, the research also revealed that even when cultures had the same values, they were prioritized differently and might be expressed differently from culture to culture.[1] So even if individuals from two cultures share similar values, their resulting behaviors can vary greatly in translation within each culture.

CULTURAL FACTORS

Although there is danger in stereotyping and automatically treating individuals according to the views and behavior of their cultural norms, many values and customs are indicative of a specific culture. Understanding these concepts, which affect the beliefs and behavior of individuals from different cultures, greatly increases the team members' ability to work together.

Individual team members bring to the team their own cultural background, beliefs, preferences, and past experience that will affect their contribution to the team and their view of the team and its members. This combination of concepts impacts the team's ability to make progress on its tasks, form productive relationships, and manage its processes to achieve successful results.

Important cultural factors include six distinct areas that affect teamwork: responsibility, participation, relationship, achievement, and time, and change.

RESPONSIBILITY

One of the most important factors affecting teamwork is responsibility. Team members take responsibility and initiative based on their cultural experience with authority—the power to direct the action of others. Any workgroup or organization has some form of power structure or hierarchy. The position of responsibility defines the status of each member of that organization. In some cultures, status is highly valued. In others it is de-emphasized, or even shunned. It depends upon the particular culture. The perception of authority directly influences the flow and effectiveness of team communication.

Team members with a more hierarchical orientation may find it extremely uncomfortable for their manager or team leader to work equally with them on a project. Most Pacific Rim cultures—such as China, Japan, Korea, Indonesia, Singapore, and Hong Kong—reflect a strong emphasis on status and power or hierarchy. They may find it too difficult to give the team leader bad news. Yet in a team environment, full participation is needed for effective teamwork. In the United States, team members increasingly view authority less as power than as a means of attaining goals. The concepts of power in most Asian nations are diametrically opposed to those in Europe and the United States. Asian power conception is characterized by a desire to avoid decision making, whereas the Western team ideal is active decision making. In Asia status rather than freedom of choice is the primary manifestation of power. With the possible exception of Japan, Asian cultures conceive of power as resting in individuals rather than in the offices they hold.

Conversely, team members from the United States, Canada, Sweden, the United Kingdom, and The Netherlands are more individualistic and entrepreneurial. The team leader may need to give direction, structure tasks, and give feedback in the context of team members' concept of responsibility.

While team collaboration means the creation of shared values and assumptions, individuals are products of their national cultures. In a look at countries in the European Union, Mary Mitchell found that the management styles and cultural characteristics of various European countries have an impact on how inclined its citizens are to work in teams.[2] Individuals from the northern European countries, including Germany, Sweden, Denmark, and The Netherlands, are the most inclined to do well in team projects. In Sweden, for example, corporate organizational structure is generally horizontal, decentralized, and democratic with less organizational hierarchy than is found in French companies. Denmark also has very flat organizational charts and a cooperative, participative management style. Danish workers would have difficulty in accepting upper management's decisions and in exercising authority over their subordinates. The Netherlands also is known for its sharing of power, as is Germany with its history of codetermination in the workplace. Dutch citizens are considered open-minded and are tolerant of differences in the culture and belief systems of other nations. This Dutch cultural characteristic, as well as the affinity for learning multiple foreign languages, makes the Dutch successful participants on intercultural teams.

One of the few exceptions to the generalization about northern European countries is Ireland's management style. In Irish companies the Chief Executive Officer is more a captain than a coach. And Irish employees typically do not know the company objectives and do not participate in management decisions.[3] With this kind of corporate culture, it is often difficult for the Irish to express their ideas or work well in a team environment. Also while Luxembourg tends to be open and adaptive to several management styles, companies in French-speaking Belgium are more structured. A popular Belgian anecdote tells of an office assistant who responded on the phone to a caller that "the boss is on holiday for two weeks, and no decisions are made in his absence."[4]

Most central European countries tend to be less enthusiastic about teamwork. However, Germany, which falls into both the northern and central regions, and nations that border the Mediterranean Sea are exceptions. Hierarchy is much more pronounced between managers and subordinates in France. They typically are not on a first name basis with superiors and have no social contact with them other than what is required in the workplace. Authority is shown the utmost respect under all circumstances.

The way in which people of unequal power interact with an organization is called *power distance.* This cultural variable was studied at length by researcher Geert Hofstede.[5] Countries ranked as having high power distance, such as France, the Philippines, Mexico, Venezuela, India, and Singapore, are more likely to believe that their superiors have greater power and are always correct, whether they are in fact correct or not. Team members from high power distance cultures are unlikely to work well in team projects requiring face-to-face openness, frankness, and feedback concerning the impact of their own or others' behavior on the group. In such countries as Austria, Israel, Denmark, New Zealand, Ireland, Sweden, Norway, and Finland, which rate low in power distance, subordinates are not so ready to accept the unequal distribution of power in the workplace.[6]

The distances that a hierarchy places between individuals can affect the degree of formality in a team culture, but more important, these distances alter the whole system of internal communication. Hierarchical distances tend to be greater in the central and southern European countries, where authority is more centralized and management more autocratic. The Portuguese culture especially encourages managers to keep information, secrets, and power to themselves and to respect distance and hierarchy, making teamwork difficult for them.[7]

RESPONSIBILITY

Since the vast majority of cultures remain very hierarchical, understanding the cultural dynamics of power and responsibility is important in the selection of team members and in understanding their interaction as work progresses. Decision-making processes vary greatly from culture to culture. Some workers look to authority figures to provide critical decisions. Others depend on majority rule or broad consensus.

PARTICIPATION

Team productivity often is affected by the members' view of participation—whether the welfare of the team is more important than the needs of each individual member. It is important to note that no culture is entirely individualistic or entirely collective. Aspects of both characteristics occur in any society, but intercultural teamwork is impacted by the degree to which team members' cultures emphasize these two contrasting characteristics.

INDIVIDUALISM

Individualism is a strong cultural variable that can make teamwork much more difficult. Individualistic societies have loose ties between people who expect to look after themselves. The American culture is one of the most pronounced examples of an individualistic society. American culture encourages the individual to excel at all tasks. Because of this emphasis, the United States leads the world in Nobel Prizes won, in the total number of new patents, in the number of new jobs created annually, and in new business starts (averaging around 700,000 per year from 1985-90).[8] Moreover the whole U.S. society is organized to benefit individuals, with an extraordinary 66.3 percent of GNP going for personal consumption. Yet once again, this extraordinary strength leaves the United States vulnerable. As America extols individualism, it also ignores the needs of the larger community upon which even the strongest individuals must depend.[9]

U.S. corporate practices are also highly individualistic. Individuals are rewarded according to their performance. In American corporations, team members are often put into competition with one another for financial incentives and promotions Other cultures, such as in Great Britian, The Netherlands, and Sweden, join the United States in basing their value systems on the welfare of the individual and then, later, form them into effective groups.

Additionally, some French team members come from an individualistic culture. These are individuals who have graduated from an educational system designed to produce stars and to teach them to prove their competencies to obtain important posts in government or industry. Other such cultures within Europe include the Italians and the French-Belgians. Rewards for individual performance do not appeal to most people from cultures in the Middle East and Asia. If team members are asked whether it matters more to select a new team member who is a team player or one who has the exact skills and knowledge for the job, their answers will be based on their own cultural background. Some team members—especially Japanese, Germans, and the French—value first the welfare of their group and then, only after the group needs are met, look to individual needs of the team.

Characteristics of individualistic cultures include speaking one's mind, feeling pride in individual accomplishment and initiative, placing a priority on tasks over relationships, acknowledging equality for all, and preferring a personal interest over group interests.

PARTICIPATION—INDIVIDUALISM

To work best with members from individualistic cultures, appeal to individual team members' interests and motives during team meetings or workgroup activities. Also, be sensitive to the possible negative impact of low achievers or high achievers. Avoid person-to-person conflict and recognize and reward individual team member performance.

COLLECTIVISM

The vast majority of people worldwide live in societies in which the interests of the group come before the interests of the individual. These societies are designated as collectivist. The family is the first group experienced, and people are integrated into strong cohesive groups from that time on. Groups in collective societies continue to protect them in exchange for unquestioning loyalty. This explains why saving face is so important in collective societies. Individuals in collective cultures are greatly embarrassed when singled out from the group, whereas individuals from individualist societies, are more concerned with self-respect. Team members may experience culture shock because of these differing cultural concepts. As a team work process is set in place and interventions are used to improve team dynamics, some members may become very uncomfortable. For example, in Saudi Arabia, men often engage in close physical contact—the complete absence of space—which would be distinctly uncomfortable for most Americans. But moving away from an Arab whom you think is too close, for instance, can be taken as an insult. As a rule, Northern cultures tend to value distance in business relationships while Southern cultures value intimacy.[10] The amount of stress that can result when these space concepts are violated should never be underestimated. Group activities that ask people to share their feelings may be difficult for individuals from cultures in which space and privacy are primary values. Participating in team experiences that may reveal educational deficits ("I have always had trouble with spelling.") or vulnerabilities ("I am afraid of speaking in front of the group.") may cause team members from collective cultures to loose *face*.[11]

Collectivism is characterized by shared responsibility and accountability, and the individuals' identities are based on the social group to which they belong. Collective interests come before individual interest, relationships are more important than tasks, harmony should always be maintained, and direct conflict and confrontation should be avoided.

PARTICIPATION—COLLECTIVISM

In interaction with team members from collective cultures, pay attention to group interests and keep these uppermost in team meetings and activities. Obtain the team leader's support; then demonstrate in the team meeting how an action will benefit the team as a whole. Avoid individually competitive situations, and constantly assess shifting team dynamics.

An example of a decision influenced by individual and collective cultural concepts is seen in the case of a Japanese manufacturing company in the United States. Company management called a team of managers together to solve the problem of high-tech equipment theft. All of the managers were American-born except for one Japanese-born manager. The U.S. managers quickly and unanimously decided on an individualistic approach: "reward the whistle-blower and punish the culprit."[12] The Japanese manager, from a group-oriented culture, had a different solution: "Reward the teams that have no theft." This dual problem-solving approach clearly demonstrates how variable cultural concepts affect GlobalWork teams and corporate management.

RELATIONSHIP

Clearly cultural dimensions impact relationships among team members, but how do relationship variables affect the teamwork process? For example, the Chinese do not want to discuss strategic ideas until the power relationships are established, and the Japanese do not like to conduct debate in public. The Swiss tend to compartmentalize their personal and business lives, keeping them separate, while the French love the art of relationships and thoroughly enjoy an elegant business lunch.[13] These cultural variables are the result of a focus on relationship. Some team members must first build a relationship and develop a level of trust with other team members before they can focus on a specific task. All members must realize that some individuals on the team will be much more committed to the task if they first have developed a relationship with their co-workers. Others may see time spent on relationship building as a waste of effort that diverts attention from the work at hand. They may not understand that relationship building can be an investment that will later pay big dividends in team process and commitment.

On the other hand, those who place a premium on relationships over tasks need to realize the importance of following an organized sequence and adhering to schedules. Not doing so would undoubtedly create irritation and frustration among teammates who expect such a focus and would possibly cause strained team relationships.

Cultural factors based on the research of Edward T. Hall and Geert Hofstede describe certain cultures as high- or low-context societies.[14] High-context cultures in Latin American and Japan, for example, place a great deal of emphasis on personal relationships. Rules, laws, and contracts are seen as less important than the bonds of personal relationships. Low context cultures—including the United States and Germany—emphasize direct communication, contracts, and the law. They are task-oriented and place a priority on getting down to business immediately. They rely on verbal communication, tolerate relatively little ambiguity, and place less emphasis on personal relationships and face-saving.

Team members from low-context cultures, such as the United States, see directness as a virtue and indirect communication a waste of time. So they often may be confronted with a controlled use of silence. By contrast, high context cultures such as those in the Pacific Rim often consider directness to be rude and offensive. They view indirect communication as a means to smooth over interpersonal differences and keep from losing face in conflict situations. American Peace Corps volunteers in the Philippines experienced this cultural paradox in how their requests were made and denied. Initially, the Americans were told to be perfectly frank in their dealings with the locals. Since the Philippine social interaction is based on interpersonal relationships, their directness was regarded as tactless and totally contrary to Filipino culture. [15] Cultural concepts of relationship also affect the individual's attitude toward conflict. Citizens from most Asian countries are very sensitive to maintaining harmony and go to what Westerners consider great lengths to save face. They also have an aversion to giving bad or unpleasant news and are unwilling to say "no" directly. Their cultural desire to save face, signifying a respectful relationship, often causes misunderstanding when business is being conducted with partners from other cultures.

Also in the Nordic countries, interpersonal conflict is something to be avoided, especially in a team setting. Words are carefully chosen so as not to offend fellow team members. In comparison, the French tend to be more aggressive in their choice of words and are prone to making extravagant statements in English, sometimes with extraordinary results. To work effectively with their groups, team leaders must understand the nuances of these cultural variables or designate a cultural translator to help them with team negotiations. Creating a team mental or visual map also will help keep the complex cultural relationships straight.

Belgian Andre Leysen provides this interesting example of cultural communication differences that affect relationships. When a Frenchman receives a letter and he is not in agreement, he does not respond. To him this sends the message, "I do not agree." On the other hand, when a German writes a letter and does not receive a response, he assumes the recipient is saying, "I agree."[16] To avoid misunderstanding through cultural variations in communication, written confirmation is important. Summarizing what was discussed by telephone in a follow-up letter or confirming what was written in a follow-up phone call clarifies the message and the intent of the communication.

RELATIONSHIP

Problems related to relationship and communication can arise based on different cultural backgrounds and different ideas about acceptable behavior in team meetings. Teams must address these issues openly and develop GlobalSolutions.

The leadership issue really starts with a GlobalVision at senior management level and the endorsement of GlobalWork teams. Team members sometimes confront problems related to process and need to come to agreement on how the team will function, make decisions, and carry out individual responsibilities. Preferences will differ based on cultures, ranging from the highly structured, technical approach of German managers to the laid-back, free-form conversational style of Italian, Spanish, and Portuguese managers who want to spend a great deal of time establishing rapport and building relationships rather than immediately dealing with details. Self-awareness of cultural beliefs and values as well as a greater understanding of the background of each team member can help in reaching a common ground.

Finally, team members should realize that the presence or absence of conflict does not necessarily mean that the team is or is not being productive. Rather, team success is determined by the team members' collective ability to work through the problems that arise, to communicate clearly with one another, and to find GlobalSolutions. To discuss and evaluate how the team is functioning every few weeks is just as crucial as it is to immediately get down to the work at hand. While initially such an approach may seem to take too much valuable time, it can build a stronger, more productive workgroup in the long-term.

This mix of cultures, religions, and social values poses endless possibilities for misunderstanding and even hostility among team members. A consistent effort to build relationships and to communicate is the best way to alleviate inevitable frictions and maintain harmonious relationships in a GlobalWork team environment.

ACHIEVEMENT

While some emphasis on form and rules may limit team members' innovative ideas, there is an inherent benefit to the German management style: an orientation toward achieving results. In addition to Germany, focus on performance objectives and final results is also strong in the United States, Sweden, Great Britain, and Denmark. European countries with the least concern for results include Greece and Portugal, where setting goals and sticking to them is difficult and where long meetings are often held without an agenda.[17]

The need to achieve and be recognized for an achievement is a driving motivator for team members from cultures that emphasize individual participation. They are prepared to take risks and go for it, and are comfortable in a team or company that provides them with this kind of opportunity. The corporation may recognize them with the rewards appropriate for their country and cultural environment such as pay for performance, promotion, status, or autonomy.

The company must also be familiar with governmental laws that often regulate reward systems in a specific country. Reward systems in France, for example, are mangled in a rigid hierarchy that can prevent advancement of workers on the basis of merit.[18] Many salaries, rights, and conditions are laid down in collective agreements to which both employers and employees are strictly bound. A two-part reward system was implemented in the mid-1980s. While one part is fixed, the other is based on merit and performance. Then an Act of 1986 has allowed companies to pay bonuses based on flexible criteria including productivity, quality improvement, cost reductions, and sales. This new system has been effective in increasing employee motivation and provides more effective rewards for outstanding performance.[19]

However, for team members from collective cultures, the motivation for achievement is acceptance and a deeper affiliation with the workgroup. These are the team members who will compete in order to show their value to their teammates, who push to achieve results for their team or company. They feel rewarded and are most satisfied when they have both security and a sense of belonging. In high context cultures, these personal relationships are much more important than monetary compensation. Even though a Nigerian manager might be promoted and given merit pay increases by his Swiss supervisor, he is apt to feel diminished motivation and disappointment if the supervisor fails to lavish personal attention on him.[20]   Global reward systems are an urgent need, yet multinational corporations are just in the beginning stages of understanding the intricacies of adapting these performance systems to each country and culture. Until appropriate models are available, managers and team leaders must be creative in meeting the needs of multiple locations and workers worldwide.

Differences in cultural concepts of appropriate rewards can cause team problems and misunderstanding. Consider the example of a new owner of a U.S. manufacturing company who wanted to reward his hard-working production employees. Most of his workers were fairly recent immigrants from Mexico and Central America. He decided to treat them to a Christmas party and spared no expense for the dinner-dance at a local hotel for all company workers and their spouses. Imagine his extreme disappointment and anger when almost no one showed up. [21]

Using a third party who spoke Spanish and understood the cultural background of the employees, he sought an explanation of his employees' behavior. He learned that most of them had never been to such a social event, that their wives did not have the appropriate clothing, and that they were afraid they would embarrass themselves or their host with inappropriate behavior. "Telling the boss directly or refusing the invitation would have seemed ungrateful and like an affront. Rather than put themselves or him in an awkward situation, they chose not to come." [22] Had the boss understood the workers' culture and family preferences, he could have planned an informal company social event that would have rewarded them appropriately and improved company relationships and teamwork.

ACHIEVEMENT

- Recognize the success of an individualistic team member with increased pay, a bonus, a promotion, or greater responsibility.
- Avoid derogatory statements about other team members' achievements and results.
- Reward the achievements of a team member who is group oriented with free time off or a special gift for the group—e.g., a restaurant meal, concert tickets, or a short team excursion.

TIME

All cultures have unique concepts of time and ways of managing it. The ways in which individuals understand and use time are often referred to by GlobalWork teams as one of the most common sources of confusion. Three areas of time affect the teamwork process. These variable cultural concepts of time are: (1) perceptions of past, present, and future, (2) scheduling of work projects, and (3) crossing time zones.

(1)   Perceptions of past, present, and future

Various cultures function according to different orientations toward the past, present, and future. Generally, cultures are either future-oriented or past-oriented. That is, today's activities will either influence future happenings or, most often, will be influenced by past events. In some societies, the past is not that important. In Japanese culture, generational cycles are very important. The older generation passes knowledge and wisdom to the younger family members. In the United States, what matters is present performance and what plans have been developed for the future. The French, on the other hand, place priority on the past and relatively less interest in the present and future. Part of the difference may be related to control over the environment, which may in turn be related to religious tradition. Mexico, for instance, is sometimes viewed as a fatalistic culture in which the past is in control of the present and future. In certain countries, such as The Netherlands, Sweden, and the United States, time is viewed as passing in a straight line, a sequence of events. Other cultures think of time more as moving in a circle, the past and present together with future possibilities. This strongly influences team activities affecting the management of agendas, appointments, decision making, schedules, lead times, and product life cycles. Especially important is whether time is *sequential*, a series of passing events, or whether it is *synchronic*, with past, present, and future all interrelated so that ideas about the future and memories of the past both shape present action.[23]

The American view of time is primarily sequential and the Japanese view is synchronic. The Japanese believe time is based on the biological clock of cycles: daily cycles, seasonal cycles, and life cycles. "The ideal is to get these all working together, waxing and waning, tensing and relaxing, all harmonized into synchronized waves of pulsing energy."[24]   One of the consistent competitive advantages attributed to the Japanese is that of strategizing long-term. In alliances with the British and Americans, the Japanese frequently offer them the opportunity to profit short-term in exchange for the long-term opportunity to develop technologies with spinoffs well into the future. The Japanese have been known to accept losses or slim profits for many years rather than abandon a technology with a long-term future. According to published reports on comparative international competitiveness by the Institute for Management Development in Lausanne, the Japanese have consistently topped the list in surveys listing countries who successfully take the long-term view.[25]

In the United States and some other countries, short-term goals are generally emphasized over long-term goals. By contrast, Japanese, Soviet, and other cultures with a more expansive perspective allow more time for carefully considered responses to initiatives.

In fact, most countries follow one of two time patterns—culturally derived concepts of time—called monochronic and polychronic. The world *monochronic* comes from the Greek and means "single time." Edward Hall, who coined the term, notes that in a monochronic culture, "scheduling is used as a classification system that orders life."[26] Monochronic time is one-track linear: individuals handle tasks one at a time, according to preset schedules. Team members who use this time pattern focus their attention on one project at a time and view time as something to be spent, lost, made up, or saved. They rigidly follow a schedule, often at the expense of personal relationships. Eva Kras explains the U.S. monochronic approach of time to a Mexican audience:

> . . ."Time is money" and since money is what business is all about, every decision, every activity, every commitment—whether at work or at home—is controlled by the clock. The executive is under constant pressure in order to meet time commitments, and much of his personal life is thereby sacrificed. Lack of punctuality is considered a disgrace, and excuses are seldom accepted. Verbal commitments are considered as binding as written ones . . . Everyday work life is often referred to as a treadmill: to succeed you must stay on it; if you step off, you are lost.[27]

To team members from polychronic cultures, a monochronic focus often presents a barrier to team effort. However, most cultures are polychronic. Generally speaking, most of Latin America, the Arabic-speaking nations, Africa (except British and Afrikaaner, South Africa), southern and western Asia, the Caribbean, and southern Europe are polychronic.

Edward Hall defined the word polychronic, also coined from the Greek, as "many or multiple time."[28] In other words, in countries with polychronic cultures, several tasks are handled simultaneously rather than in scheduled succession. In polychronic cultures, a task is usually completed even if it is necessary to go beyond the time scheduled for doing so. Polychronic time is multitrack circular and allows many things to happen simultaneously, with no particular end in sight. Scheduling is considered approximate rather than specific, and greater emphasis is placed on personal interaction than on schedules.

(2)   Scheduling of work projects

Whenever time orientation is a variable within a cross-cultural team, time decisions must be negotiated. One of the first decisions a team must make is the determination of a local *team time culture*. For example, Americans will try to do jobs faster, and the Japanese and Germans will be more concerned with the overall synchronization of separate tasks. Americans will analyze before they integrate. Germans will integrate before they analyze, and always consider the part in the context of the whole. In the process of developing a team time culture, the work values and time orientations of every team member should be explicitly acknowledged. This can prevent misunderstandings about punctuality and reliability. Team members must be allowed some freedom to proceed at their own pace within agreed time commitments.

These different orientations to time can make the planning process difficult for everyone involved. Project interruptions, postponements, and missed deadlines are indicative of high-context (synchronic time) cultures and extremely annoying to low-context (sequential time) workers. Team projects should be designed with a fine balance between flexibility and on-time performance to accommodate both cultural concepts. Time criteria must be explicitly established among team members at the outset, and adapted as needed during the project. Commitments can be seen as agreements to complete specific action items.

Time orientations have great relevance also in cross-functional teaming. Functional—as opposed to professional—cultures are the roles, practices, and habits associated with a particular work function, often defined by departments, such as finance, sales, marketing, personnel, and research and development. Functional cultures, no less than primary cultures, tend to be more or less monochronic or polychronic and oriented to past, present, or future. R&D people typically have a long-term perspective, which is reinforced by the tendency to measure their productivity by the frequency of bits of ideas. Accounting, on the other hand, must have a short-term, incremental point of view and a present-tense orientation to remain on track. People with polychronic-oriented functions, as in marketing, sales, and advertising, are better able to blend into cross-functional teams because of their ability to handle simultaneous activity. Monochronic, present-oriented individuals, such as accounting and information systems specialists, find teamwork much more daunting.

(3)   Crossing time zones

When distance is added to the time equation, collaboration becomes extremely complex. And yet these challenges are increasingly the reality of GlobalWork teams. Global customer relations and service, as well as sales and marketing strategies have to be customized to local cultural conditions.

In some high-tech companies, groups from different geographic areas of the world collaborate on simultaneous projects within their own work hours and also across time zones. These team members are connected to one another by computer networks or Wide Area

Networks (WANs). For example, a team member in Pittsburgh will begin a product design. At the end of the U.S. work day, a team member on the computer network in India will continue the project as work is shared around the world and around the clock, overcoming the barriers of time and space.

Examples of such long distance teamwork are described by Bill Johnson, a department manager in the Design Automation Division of Texas Instrument's Semiconductor Group. The purpose of this division is to develop and support software that is used by integrated circuit designers located with TI worldwide. The software developers also are located throughout the world and communicate largely through Wide Area Networks (WANs) via written messages, since English is the team language used, and is a secondary language for all team members.[29] This communication is augmented by occasional verbal/visual means, such as phone calls, video conferences, and face-to-face visits. Similarly, the integrated circuit designers at TI also design data via the WAN as needed. Key to the success of these teams are the network and the common language.

An increasingly popular kind of business software—known as groupware—also is helping company employees in any industry share files, send electronic mail, schedule team meetings, and edit documents. At Frito-Lay Inc., officials credit groupware for speeding the introduction of its larger, rounder Doritos tortilla chips in December 1994. Instead of playing telephone tag to seek approval for a change in packaging, team members could view the design on their computer screens and immediately suggest changes. Managers could track the progress of the chip redesign by computer rather than by distributing interoffice from their Plano, Texas, corporate headquarters and waiting for written responses.[30] Frito-Lay is communicating electronically with workers in 40 U.S. plants and with suppliers and retailers as well. Groupware is dominated by Lotus Development Corporation's Notes software program, and the workgroup software business which nearly doubled to $729 million in 1994 is expected to reach $3.5 billion by 1998.[31]

CHANGE

Another cultural factor that affects teamwork is the tolerance for risk and rapid change or, as Hofstede refers to it, uncertainty avoidance. While the British tend to be comfortable with uncertainties and not knowing every detail in an operation or project, the Germans, the German Swiss, and the Flemish Belgians tend to be the most risk-averse of the Europeans. Their attachment to rules and details conveys their strong desire to control uncertainty and to lessen the unpredictable aspects of a project by building up a list of small certainties.[32]

Extreme uncertainty creates unbearable anxiety, and this anxiety can greatly impact the team process. Feelings of uncertainty and the ways team members cope with them are personal and culturally learned. These feelings are transferred and reinforced through the family, educational systems, and the government of a particular country. They lead to collective patterns of behavior in one culture which may seem unreasonable to members of other cultures. This fear of uncertain or unknown situations is expressed in a need for predictability and for written and unwritten rules.

Countries with strong uncertainty avoidance tend to have more precise laws. Germany, for example, has laws in the event that all other laws may become unenforceable. On the other hand, Great Britain does not even have a written constitution. The strength of uncertainty avoidance in a given culture also depends on its cultural concept of individualism or collectivism and strongly influences a team member's ability to weather change.

The Center for Intercultural Training and Education (Cite) lists suggestions on how to interact with team members who have a low uncertainty avoidance and, therefore, are more comfortable with change and risk taking. The suggestions include:

- Expect people to get down to business fairly quickly.
- Do not hesitate to disagree as long as you play fair . . . avoid the *low blow.*

- Risk taking is acceptable as long as the action is not too dangerous or likely to cause someone else harm.
- Expect people to be warm and friendly, but do not expect this to mean they will become long-term friends or trusted associates.
- Expect people to easily abandon the rules if it is in their interest. However, know the "unspoken" rules of behavior and make sure you know what is the acceptable range of behavior.[33]

For those team members who have a high uncertainty avoidance and a corresponding discomfort with change and risk taking, follow these suggestions:

- Take time to build relationships before beginning business. People do not like to conduct business in the early stages of a relationship.
- A highly emotional conversation between associates may not mean disagreement. Do not intervene.
- At the beginning, expect people to be formal, polite, correct, but not especially friendly or open, since this makes one vulnerable.
- Do not be surprised by what seem to be excessive rules of procedure.
- When giving presentations, give people much more data than you think is needed.[34]

TIME AND CHANGE

Teams should strive to balance the members' variable concepts of time and change for successful team productivity. GlobalWork teams should pay close attention to these six cultural factors and the corresponding variations among their members' behavior. With this understanding, they can then develop a team work process that meets the needs of all.

Figure 4-2 visually displays a comparison of the five major cultures of the AOC Management Group project that can be used in team facilitation.

FIGURE 4-2

Analysis Of AOC TeamWork Cultural Factors

CULTURAL FACTORS	Egypt	Australia	United Kingdom	Norway	India
Responsibility					
Authority Focus	Leader	Individual	Individual	Individual	Leader
Communication	Indirect	Direct	Direct	Direct	Indirect
Participation					
Group or Individual Focus	Group	Individual	Individual	Individual	Group
Individual Space Needed	Less	More	More	More	More
Relationship					
Task or Relationship Focus	Relationship	Task	Task	Relationship	Relationship
Achievement					
Performance and Rewards	Group	Individual	Individual	Individual	Group
Time					
Short- or Long-Term Focus	Short	Long	Long	Short	Long
Punctuality	Less Important	Important	Important	Less Important	Important
Change					
Risk Taking or Avoidance	Avoid	Risk	Risk	Avoid	Avoid

The cultural factors discussed in this chapter are based on stereotypical information of each specific culture. Although most should resist stereotyping and automatically treating them according to their native country's cultural concepts. On occasion team members may appear to be culturally adapted, but threads of their values may still remain. For example, in a college class, a young Asian woman's visible behavior indicated she was adapted to western culture. However, when the students applauded her facilitation skills in a team exercise, she became very quiet. Later, she explained that in her culture it is embarrassing to be praised in public. So, even though in many respects she had adopted American behaviors, she still retained certain cultural values of her own heritage.[35]

THE SYNTHESIS OF CULTURES

A word of caution: Team members should never seem to *go native*—adopting the local culture at the expense of their own culture.

Christopher A. Bartlett and Sumantra Ghosal recommended training program elements for global managers. These are important points for cross-cultural teams as well.

- **Legitimize diversity**, maintaining a dynamic balance. Develop flexibility in problemsolving. Highlight the advantages of incorporating the points of view of all cultures, not just emulating a pattern that has worked in the past but is based on obsolete hierarchical organizational structures. Manage complexity.

- **Recognize cultural differences** and overcome cultural barriers. Importance of pride of heritage in all cultures.

- **Encourage transnational innovations**. Work together for mutual benefit—the inevitable give and take in such an environment.

- **Allow input** from all facilities into the company's vision/mission statements to insure that all affected operations' knowledge will be incorporated and to guarantee buy-in of all parties. Result becomes a personal as well as a corporate goal.

- **Create an atmosphere** in which employees work as teams, share ideas and resources, and have common values—where the people make it happen.

- **Integrate local worldwide operations** into a corporate network for new growth, development, and worldwide competition. Identify characteristics of transnational individuals and organizations, the lessons of history, management implications, and challenges. The traditional vs. emerging change process models.

- **Redefine the manager's role** in a transnational context.

- **Encourage people who train together** to build bonds and personal relationships—a network of informal contacts.[36]

Two international corporations reflect these points in their management philosophies: PepsiCo Foods & Beverages International and Unilever.

PEPSICO FOODS & BEVERAGES INTERNATIONAL

With 81,000 employees worldwide, John R. Fulkerson, vice president organization and management development, points to seven common global imperatives shared by PepsiCo Foods & Beverages International: global mindset/synergies, great products/quality, customer focus/service, sales/operating excellence, exciting product news/quality, innovation/ideas, aligned/skilled/empowered people and organizations.[37] PepsiCo Foods & Beverages International's management team consists of 300 executives from 45 countries. Two-thirds of these executives are non-American, and 75 percent of offshore executives are non-American. Also, four of their six senior field presidents are from India, Peru, Mexico, and Canada. These field presidents oversee the manufacturing and distribution of products in 180 plus countries.

"We see that the organization of the future," states Fulkerson, "can best be described as: global, competency based, virtual/fluid, empowered, decentralized, and connected."[38]   He believes that the future of our global village is characterized by:

- Sharing ideas
- Changing paradigms
- Letting go of outmoded ways of thinking
- Movement of people, products, and technology

The corporation constantly strives to be results and customer focused and value driven. "PepsiCo wants to be seen as a company of integrity as our workforce grows and learns together," he continues, "and one of the ways these goals can be achieved is through managing diversity." The company must (1) celebrate diversity, (2) make it an ongoing, everyday part of the organization's fabric, (3) use diversity in it's broadest sense, (4) accept the differences, (5) be ruthless about the sharing of best practices, and (6) have a childlike wonder about what is new.[39] In managing a multinational, multicultural workforce there are 17 areas that executives must review and question their ability to meet the challenges:

- Multinational Teams
- Global Competencies
- Worldwide Meetings
- Multicultural Training for Certain Managers
- Multicultural Training Uniformly Done
- Language Training for Internationals
- Language Training for Postings Offshore
- International Interns
- International Succession Plans
- International Development Assignments
- Worldwide Vision/Values Statements
- Worldwide Surveys
- Worldwide Performance Management
- Diversity Expat Pool
- Track Expat Adaptability
- Cross-cultural Training for Expats
- Cross-cultural Training for Sales Reps who live in the United States but work outside.

In managing these areas, Fulkerson sees high performance leadership as a must. It is "more than a management tool or a standard of excellence. It's a passion for creating dramatic changes that fundamentally improve PepsiCo's competitive and financial position . . . and for sustaining momentum by developing and empowering others to do the same." [40]

UNILEVER

Unilever is often described as one of the foremost transnational companies. CEO and Co-Chairman Floria A. Maljers explains how the factors outlined by Bartlett and Ghosal led to their present structure: a matrix of individual managers around the world who nonetheless share a common vision and understanding of corporate strategy. In their international company, incorporating both unity and diversity, they have a consistent, long-standing policy of managing people rather than simply analyzing problems.

> We look for people who can work in teams and understand the value of cooperation and consensus. We expect managers to gain experience in more than one country or product line. Through the training programs, experiences are shared by trainees creating an informal network of equals who know one another well and usually continue to meet and exchange experiences. Such an exchange is particularly important in an organization that has an extremely diverse group of international managers. The company has focused on the importance of linking decentralized units through a common corporate culture. We have realized over time that the transnational way of working helps to maintain common standards of behavior in our far-flung units. In other words, we strive for unity in diversity. [41]

An effective team is one in which all the members and tasks are recognized as important, and no matter how disparate the team members are in terms of their cultures, skills, and motivation, each needs to be able to accept that they all have something to contribute. It is imperative for effective teamwork that cultural variables be embraced and understood. By understanding and harnessing the multiple cultures within a GlobalWork team, the team can capitalize on the cultural strengths of each team member. "An automobile, for example, might best get its steel from Korea, its engines from Germany, its electronics from Japan, its leather and mahogany from

Britain, and its safety systems from Sweden," explain Charles Hampden-Turner and Fons Trompenaars.[42] Taking the time and effort to translate culture to culture will strengthen the GlobalWork team's collaboration and will greatly impact corporate success in the global marketplace.

Chapter 5

Competencies for GlobalWork Teams

Competencies for GlobalWork Teams

As strategic alliances define the organization's form and structure, global competencies are becoming critical for survival and success. One of the most crucial competencies for employees today is GlobalThink. "All leaders are today, or will be in the future, global," says Corporate Vice President Patrick Canavan of Motorola.[1]

MOTOROLA

Canavan defines global as being anywhere in the organizational web, with any geographic scope of responsibility. Global is defined by the environment and not by personal time/space movement or by a global/worldwide position title. As Motorola director of global leadership and organizational development, Canavan understands that global leaders—whether they are executives, managers, or team leaders—must evidence transcultural competence through:

- Interest in different cultures and business practices
- Nonjudgmental initial interaction with difference
- Conceptual understanding of the power of difference
- Modeling of product/service diversity related to culture

These global leaders are advocates for their geography and are able to learn from traveling and interacting with travelers and employees from other areas of the world. Leadership characteristics that Canavan believes are important for success globally are:

- Physical stamina
- The ethnographic data collection skills of cultural anthropologists

- An expanding repertoire of behavior
- Sense of humor
- Personal belief in life as a journey
- Commitment to the greatness of their organization
- A deep connection to a higher purpose being facilitated by participation in the organization

"Global Leadership is not a state, it is a process—and all members of the organization in positions of leadership are in the process," Canavan continues. "Leadership *per se* is the evidence of thought, word and deed within the culture of the organization which contributes to survival and growth of the system. This requires occasional acts of bravery and risk which alter the course of the system through influencing and modeling the behavior of others."[2]

The interaction that occurs between members of multicultural teams can create either positive or negative energy. The key issue in forming successful teams is how to manage the energy productively—to ensure that the teams capitalize rather than underutilize or waste the positive energies of their members. The GlobalWork team needs to create cultural synergy for cooperation and collaborative action. When team cultural synthesis is successful, the result is cultural synergy.

"There has to be a fit between people and their organizational culture if synergy is to occur. In the future global managers will direct more effort toward promoting that match," Philip R. Harris and Robert T. Moran suggest.[3] One strategy is to select team leaders who, because of their functions and previous performance on projects, task forces, or product teams, will fit well on a particular team.

TEAM CULTURAL INTERACTION

The interplay and influence of cultural factors and national parameters on the function of team members was discussed in Chapter 4. As Figure 5-1 illustrates, another critical influence on team performance is the competencies of both team leaders and team members.

FIGURE 5-1

Synthesis of Cultures
For GlobalWork Teams

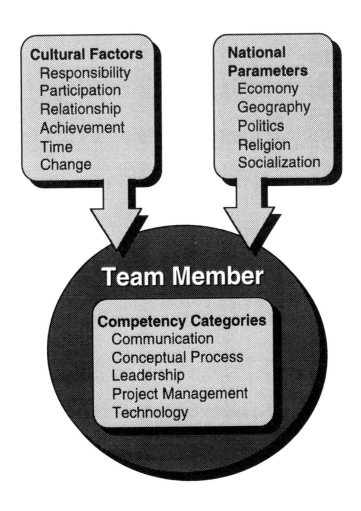

Figure 5-2 lists examples of critical competencies required. However, the level of skill required in each competency is dependent upon the function of the project team.

FIGURE 5-2

Competency Categories

Communication Skills
- Listening
- Verbal (Interpersonal and Presentation)
- Nonverbal
- Writing
- Language

Conceptual Process Skills
- Problem solving/decision making
- Negotiating
- Open minded
- Innovative
- Perceptive
- Anticipating
- Discerning

Technical Skills
- Computer
- Task and function specific

Leadership Skills
- Tolerant
- Flexible
- Persuasive
- Consensus building
- Coaching
- Change oriented
- Patient

Project Management Skills
- Delegating
- Scheduling
- Forecasting
- Strategic planning
- Process focused
- Prioritizing
- Interviewing
- Bottom-line focused

It is critically important for leaders to have as many of the competencies as possible. However, in today's specialization era, team members can complement team leaders' skills if they lack some of the competencies. Since no one individual can perform well in all of these skill areas, training for members and leaders is crucial to increase their skill levels.

Competencies for Team Leadership

Developing the capacity to create and sustain global teams is the business challenge of the 21st Century, and the challenge rests largely on the shoulders of those who are designated as team leaders. Selecting the right team leaders is critical. Generally speaking, these leaders should have a:

- Proven track record in the ability to learn and to coach others.
- Thorough understanding of the project and of each work area and its relationship to other areas and to each team member. This knowledge allows them to maximize the leverage of the team effort to the project requirements.

Team leaders need to pay careful attention to group process—the complex dynamics that block or open the doors to productive teamwork. They must constantly focus on the team's goals. Leaders should synthesize the diverse cultural perspectives and requirements of individual team members to accomplish team goals. Although technical skills and project experience are important, the most critical skill required to achieve group goals is interpersonal skills. Team leaders must be culturally astute, flexible, and able to deal with a great deal of ambiguity. They should recognize that cultures have values and beliefs that team members will not violate, nor should they. Leaders must be able to deal with diverse cultural perspectives without compromising the integrity of their team.

C. K. Prahalad, professor of business administration at the University of Michigan, lists eight demands of a global manager or team leader:

- Interpersonal, intercultural competence
- Capacity to work at a distance
- Language skills
- Capacity to manage ambiguity and stress
- Personal excellence and discipline
- Expertise and perspective

- Capacity to work in multiple teams
- Curiosity, capacity to learn and to forget
- Rethinking loyalty—company, profession, family country, religious values
- Accountability and trust
- Physical stamina[4]

The teamwork process will also move much faster if team leaders are multilingual and can provide each subgroup with directions in their own language. In addition, team leaders should have cultural awareness and understand the value systems of all team members' cultures and be able to differentiate their motivation. Since, team member responses could be anywhere between apathy on the negative side to action on the positive side, leaders must help move team members from fear and hostility—collision—to a mutual point of acceptance and trust—coexistence. Then they must motivate them to collaboration—an interest in processing ideas and information.

Leaders not only must move the team to action, they must:

- Assess the team members' skills needed to do the job
- Handle personal agendas on an individual level
- Diffuse perceived inequities, explaining to team members what they will gain or lose by results
- Allow diverse groups to gain perspective on why projects are being done a certain way
- Assess team attitude on each aspect of team functions, (i.e., assignments, reports, deadlines, and conflict resolution)
- Focus their teams on outcomes to get more willing compliance

Team leaders must also develop process facilitation skills. They must have a high tolerance for ambiguity and have the capacity to coordinate across time, distance, and cultures. They must manage teams whose members speak different languages, have different beliefs about authority, time, and decision making, have access to different technological capabilities and supports, and bring a variety of direct and indirect relationships to the company and the mission.

And they must do so even though members often have little time to work face-to-face and in some cases never even meet one another.

Team leaders must be aware of what each individual team member needs personally and as an individual team contributor. They can allow for individual contributions but should know when and how to bring the team together. As a result, leaders of transnational teams must be more skilled to deal with diverse concepts and ideologies to achieve team performance. A team leader's ability to influence the team has to be better than a manager's, who can influence from a position of authority.

COMPETENCIES FOR TEAM MEMBERS

In order to be a team leader, the leader must have followers, and team followers expect their leader to communicate the level of vision, risk, and responsibility that is required of them for their assignments. An effective strategy for GlobalWork teams is to look at the cultural mix of potential team members and the competencies needed by those who will be placed on the team. However, selecting members for intercultural teams based on competencies is a new area for most companies. No best way has been designed. The targeted competencies must accommodate the cultural conditions, geographical distribution, technological possibilities, and operational mission unique to the team. And even with the most careful selection, every team will be dynamic and will develop its own team culture in its own way.

Member selection to a team role depends on various types of competencies. Traditionally, companies select team members according to their technical expertise without any consideration of their ability to work together. Then they wonder why teams do not accomplish their goals.

COMMUNICATION SKILLS

The analysis of the team communication process is essential in meeting the challenge of working globally. First, team members should use their skills to listen and observe to determine if the culture is high or low context. Then, they should pay special attention to the work done by an individual in the culture. For example, with an Arab, the conversation might be full of fantastic exaggerations and metaphors, leap from one topic to another in what some have described as loops of thought that move away from the topic and back again more poetically than logically. Understanding this communication style is important in building a team relationship.[5]

When Americans work with Koreans, Thais, and Saudis (all high-context cultures) their direct approach, insistence on data, and need to come to a quick decision are often seen as insincere. Americans who fail to demonstrate interest in the person from a high-context culture miss the opportunity afforded by the practice of social activities such as sharing lunch or a round of golf. Business can be integrated into the relationship only after a strong personal foundation of trust is established.[6]

All teams must accept the fact that it is natural to experience some difficulties—especially if the team is multicultural. Rather than viewing these differences as insurmountable, one technique is to categorize the difficulties and then attempt to address them collectively with the group. Conflict resolution and teambuilding activities will help overcome the differences in low- and high-context cultures interaction.

CONCEPTUAL PROCESS SKILLS

Most team members need to belong, to be part of the team, to be valued and respected. So, an effective team is one in which all the members are accepted as true members of the team and have tasks that are recognized as important. No matter how disparate the team members are in terms of their background, skills, and motivation, each one needs to accept that the others have something to contribute. Differences between team members should, in fact, be welcomed. Teams made up of members with very similar characteristics rarely produce innovative results. By acknowledging its diverse skills, a team can maximize the resources it has. In some cases the available skills for a task will not be required or some of the skills will be more needed than others. However, it is still important that all team members know that their contributions are valued.[7]

Team members should be open minded and willing to consider other viewpoints and possibilities rather than being closed minded or locked into their own previous conceptions. They should also be flexible in responding to new ideas and different perceptions. These competencies can be addressed first in the selection process by reviewing job candidates not only for their skills and work-related experience, but also for their ability to get along with others. Judging on the basis of individual interviews and references from previous employers, management can then hire employees who welcome diversity and are willing to work on a team.

Team members are not required to become close friends or to even like each other. They do not have to eat lunch together or share social activities with members of different job functions or cultures. They can work side by side as team members and not even be required to talk. However, any emotions or barriers between team members should not be allowed to interfere with the work of the team. If such behavior continually interferes with team efforts, these team members should be switched to other team assignments.

Corporations cannot expect all team members to be catalysts or change agents, nor do they need them to be. At some levels they just need someone to perform a predictable task over and over and do it well. An example of this type of job is that of an equipment operator on the AOC Management Group project.

TECHNICAL SKILLS

Of course, the technical expertise of potential team members is the first competency requirement. When cross-functional and multicultural teams are formed, the choice of communications technology has major implications. Team members must be able to use communication tools to promote the flow of information. Clearly, some linear communication tools, such as e-mail and fax, operate at a low-context cultural level—which is appropriate for direct data transfer and simple point-to-point communications. However, these tools are inadequate for the elaborate emotional requirements of high-context cultures. Video and audio conferencing come closer to meeting these needs, although nothing really substitutes for face-to-face encounters.

CORE COMPETENCIES

Competencies are defined as individual skills for the purpose of this study. However, companies also need core competencies that enhance their corporate competitiveness. Gary Hamel and C. K. Prahalad in their book, *Competing for the Future: Breakthrough Strategies for Seizing Control of Your Industry and Creating the Markets of Tomorrow,* describe core competencies as the bundles of skills and technologies that enable a company to provide a particular benefit to customers. These core competencies are a composite of individual team members' skills or competencies. Hamel and Prahalad propose there are three conditions if a corporation wants to have core competencies:

- You have to train team members in new skills and have to train them constantly in those skills.
- These competencies must be continuously used and reconfigured if you want them to be sustained and nurtured.
- To develop these competencies, groups must include teams of employees who not only cut across functions but organizational levels as well.[8]

Although teams may not be identified by specific core competencies, the individual team member competencies can greatly enhance the corporation's ability to build its core competencies.

At their VästerÅs location, ASEA Brown Boveri (ABB) developed competency matrices identifying what competencies each working group needs to cope with new tasks. It identifies what competencies employees already have and what development is planned. All team members have competency plans that are reviewed in talks with their managers. ABB's goal is to set aside 150 hours per employee, per year for competency development. The training includes areas such as job rotation, benchmarking, training on the job, participation in technical development or theoretical education.[9]

COMPETENCY TRAINING

"Tapping into the forces of both globalization and learning organizations is a process and strategy that has barely begun," note Michael Marquardt and Angus Reynolds in *The Global Learning Organization*.[10] International corporations must develop global human resource strategies and training for intercultural management and team leadership. Human resource managers can no longer adapt the past to be ready for the future. They will have to break molds in order to assist line managers to survive and grow globally. These changes will affect all activities including how teams are selected, how performance is measured, and how reward systems are structured. "Taking a backseat is no longer acceptable. You have to get in there and take risks," explains Rick A. Swaak, vice president for international human resource services of the National Foreign Trade Council.[11] He continues:

> It is exciting to see current practitioners flock to seminars and symposiums to tackle issues of cost containment and business competitiveness head-on and to come up with solutions that reveal a deep understanding of business and the world we are competing in. It is also encouraging to notice the influx of neophytes into the

profession who have the ability to look at things from a different perspective and who are adding immense value to the formation of best practices in almost all areas of international human resources.[12]

According to Peter Senge in *The Fifth Discipline*, "Work must become a continual process of learning how to create our future rather than react to our past."[14] The learning environment must also include team learning. Continuous learning and competency training are moving into the forefront to expand the capabilities of teams. Many corporations now call their training organizations universities, "suggesting much more than training: a broad focus, concern for complete development of all employees, research, connection to the larger education community, and leading-edge thinking," Marcia Atkinson notes in "Build Learning into Work."[14]

Universities also are offering innovative international programs. The University of Michigan has instituted a five-week global leadership program that takes participants to China for two weeks where they are required to develop a business plan in a totally alien environment. Additionally, many universities are engaging in joint training programs with countries. For example, Stanford University started a joint program in 1992 with Mexico's Monterrey Institute of Technology and Higher Education.[15]

"Individual learning, at some level, is irrelevant for organizational learning," continues Senge. "Teams must tap the potential for many minds to be more intelligent than one mind . . . though team learning involves individual skills and areas of understanding, it is a collective discipline."[16] Team learning requires respect for education within the workgroup.

Effective Meetings Training at Sequent Computer Systems is one example of team learning in action. As John Coné explains:

> Competitive organizations need to embed learning into the course of work, making it transparent, much like the Help File for your computer software. For instance, instead of conducting separate Effective

Meeting classes, our strategy is to teach specific employees to be expert observers and coaches, then place enough of them in actual business meetings to counsel meeting leaders during breaks about how implementing an activity might improve meeting progress. In other words, we're training in real time.[17]

According to the American Society for Training and Development's Benchmarking Forum Data Report, which summarizes the best practices in world-class workplace training companies, the average cost of training per employee in 1992 amounted to $1,235, or 2.8 percent of payroll.[18]

Software house Infosys Technologies Ltd. depends on teamwork throughout its organization. The Bangalore (India)-based Infosys resembles California rivals more than India's traditional hierarchical behemoths. Deputy Managing Director Nandan Nilekani explains, "Depending on the job, teams form, do the work, and then disband."[19] Additionally, Fiat spent $64 million training workers and engineers to operate in independent, multiskilled teams. Factory workers and office staff now labor together under the same roof. Top-down decision making is dead, says Maurizio Magnabosco, Fiat Auto's personnel chief. "Problems are solved by teams actually working on production."[20]

Anglo-Dutch multinational Unilever provides an example of the importance of interdisciplinary teamwork. Floris Maljers, chairman of the board, explains that the company has experienced more changes in the last six to eight years than it had in the previous 50 years and that one of the reasons the company has survived is that people increasingly understand the need to be flexible in their organizational behavior. Part of that flexibility is in the proliferation of project teams.

> "We choose a group of people of all disciplines and departments who may have never worked together and say to them, for example, find (a) a new toothpaste that is (b) good for health and (c) can be launched all over Europe as soon as possible. The team members speak to people all over the company and work together under a project director to solve the problem. We call these 'project teams' because we use people

who are not normally doing that type of work and release the creativity
of the new combinations of people, problems and ideas."[21]

The most significant fact that corporations must recognize is that
achieving goals through workgroup teams is a process, and the
process will always be a moving target. There are no fixed formulas
for success. A constant need for evaluation and change will always
exist to meet the demands of the global marketplace.

Chapter 6

A Model for GlobalWork Teams

Chapter 6

A Model for GlobalWork Teams

Forming productive cross-cultural teams is a complex process. To accomplish project goals through GlobalWork teams, the workgroup must progress from being a collection of individuals with cultural differences to an effective working unit—from collision to coexistence in the team's formative stage, to individuals operating as a collaborative GlobalWork team.

TEAM MEMBER PROGRESSION

Figure 6.1 illustrates this four phase progression.

FIGURE 6-1

Team Member Progression

	Team Formations		Team Operation	
	Phase 1	*Phase 2*	*Phase 3*	*Phase 4*
Primary Orientation	Self-centered	Awareness Shared	Team Contributor	Team/Company Shared
Technology	Proprietary	Selectively Shared	Team Shared	Collaboratively Shared
Influence on Company	Small	Small + Open	Larger	Largest
	COLLISION —— COEXISTENCE		**—— COLLABORATION**	

Phase 1

All teams members bring with them to the team their own cultural perspectives. Early in the formation of the team, members must begin to understand their own cultures, values, and workstyles before they can work effectively with others.

Phase 2

After self-awareness, members must gain awareness and an understanding of the cultural perspectives of others. Corporations should provide cultural awareness and multicultural training to increase trust, communication, and cooperation among team members to get work done. In this way, individuals begin to see how their work preferences are similar to or different from other team members. This allows them to work alongside other team members as they move toward greater understanding and cooperation.

Phase 3

At this stage, cooperation takes on increasing importance. As trust builds, team members are more willing to share their knowledge and technology with each other. The team's focus shifts from themselves to accomplishing team goals.

Phase 4

Cross-cultural dynamics influence the team as it is now transformed into a collaborative working unit. It incorporates the company's vision and strategy into its kinetic team culture and contributes to organizational goals. As new members become part of the unit, the workgroup must reconfigure its work process to incorporate new perspectives.

How does a corporation get work done amidst the collisions of cultural differences in the formation and operations of teams?

Corporations have met these challenges with a number of different strategies. Maxus Energy and Holderbank are examples of global corporations who have creatively met the challenge.

MAXUS ENERGY

Maxus Energy is an example of a company that has risen to the challenge of bringing teams from collision to collaboration. It is an oil and gas exploration and production company based in Dallas, Texas. The company is an operator of a Production Sharing Contract for Pertamina, the Indonesian government's oil company, in the development of the vast oil resources of the country. Maxus is the second largest producer of oil in Indonesia.

Typically, oil production declines rapidly after the first few years of production.[1] In 1985 production over the next several years was expected to decline by a total of 14 percent. The company, working with Bob Sneider, a consultant on teams in the oil patch, initiated a multidisciplinary team approach to attempt to reduce the severe production decline. As a result of implementing the teams, the company's production from old fields was virtually flattened over the next 10 years and significant amounts of reserves were added.

Numerous issues had to be addressed in the development of the teams, which represent many cultures as well as technical disciplines. With 17,508 islands (6,000 of which are inhabited), Indonesia is the world's largest archipelago. The geographical separation of the people promotes varied subcultures in addition to the national culture. Some are mild-natured and others are more aggressive. Additional cultural influences come from significant numbers of Asian people of varied national origins in the population as well as the presence of Dutch, Australian, English, Canadian, and U.S. expatriates.

Other key cultural differences at issue are:

- The view of the individual and the community—American individualism is in sharp contrast with the general Indonesian group mentality. [See Chapter 4: participation factor, individualism and collectivism.]

- The view of class and leadership — The American view of equal opportunity and earned leadership is very different from the Indonesian culture based on age and seniority. [See Chapter 4: responsibility factor.]

- The style and method of communication — Americans are more direct, formal, and confrontational than Indonesians who tend to be more subtle and indirect, respectful, and accommodating. [See Chapter 4: relationship factor, direct and indirect communication.] The Indonesian style is the result of hundreds of years of rule by colonial influences and Pancasila, which is the national ideology. The five inseparable and mutually qualifying fundamental principles of this ideology are:

  1. Belief in the One Supreme God
  2. A just and civilized humanity
  3. The unity of Indonesia
  4. Democracy led by the wisdom of deliberations among representatives
  5. Social justice for all the people of Indonesia

- The view of work and the company — Americans are task-oriented and have a single loyalty to the company, while Indonesians tend to be relationship-driven with multiple loyalties to the company and the government. [See Chapter 4: relationship or task focus.]

In setting up a culturally relevant team structure, Maxus established the following guidelines:

- Promote representation of varied functions and cultures.

- Define the role of the multidisciplinary teams. (Maxus refers to these teams as Asset Management Teams or AMTs.) The roles of the teams, the team leaders, and the team managers were identified and guidelines were developed. (Charts are shown on pages 118-122.)

- Establish clear guidelines for team function and operation including goals and objectives, specific times for required meetings, and deadlines for reports.

- Monitor the team's progress through quarterly updates, annual reports, and electronic databases to monitor progress and communicate areas of concern.

- Be hesitant to make changes to team decisions, and do so only after very careful examination and team input.

- Provide support as follows:

  - Technical support. Tools to get the job done, expertise to minimize wasted effort, and computer databases and communication software to expedite processes and improve communication.

  - Verbal support. Talk about the teams. Recognize the efforts being made at every opportunity and celebrate the accomplishments.

  - Monetary support. (This area is currently being addressed. Provide individual as well as team rewards and a bonus system to recognize teamwork and effort.)

  - Decision making. Give as many decisions to the team as practical and operationally possible. If management decides to change a decision, respect the team by giving the members an opportunity to discuss and defend their decision.

Maxus's team approach has been very successful. In 1992 the company evaluated their team guidelines for the year to determine what they had or had not done well. On the plus side, they had set up teams with at least one technical expert in each discipline in every AMT. They had given clear objectives for AMTs, limited the size of teams to 10 members, and had given leaders the responsibility to experiment with structure and format.[2]

They also found some activities on the minus side, which they corrected:

- They had assigned people to more than one AMT and found that was not effective.

- They had formed too many AMTs with limited scope, so in 1992 they decreased the number of AMTs and enlarged the boundaries based on geographical areas/geological setting versus fields. This allowed an

AMT to have several fields and assign responsibilities within the AMT. The number of AMTs was based on the number of experts available, production, the number of wells, and geological setting.

- They had not required AMTs to meet on a regular basis and changed this so that they now meet at least once a week.

- They had located offices in the building based on functional groups and not by AMTs. In the future this will be corrected.

The company has identified additional issues that will require improvement such as the need to focus on key issues, establish meeting agendas and eliminate time wasters, and move people around less to maintain continuity.

The following are charts showing the guidelines developed for teams, leaders, and managers.[3]

ASSET MANAGEMENT TEAMS*

Objective: Efficiently and effectively optimize production and reserves from producing areas and serve as a training vehicle for technical as well as leadership skills.

The primary responsibility of each AMT is to optimize results by applying multidisciplinary expertise to all technical evaluations in the given geographical area of responsibility.

The AMT is:	The AMT is not:
• A multidisciplinary team. All disciplines needed to perform the required task are represented.	• Competing disciplines working the same area.
• Self-directed. Leader and manager serve a support function.	• Managed/directed by one person.
• Optimally sized (8-15).	• Too large (difficult to focus). Too small (lacking functional representation).
• Focused by clear self-generated goals and objectives that had management's input and agreement.	• Working on multiple conflicting agendas from functional departments.

The AMT does:	The AMT does not:
• Set aggressive goals and objectives with input and agreement from management.	• Receive goals to achieve without input (top down).
• Meet regularly to discuss progress and jointly work out problems.	• Only meet to solve major problems.
• Promote cross-functional solutions and input from all members (synergy).	• Restrict participation to individual's discipline and expertise (for example, geologist—geology; product engineer—workovers).
• Seek technical audit from functional groups (i.e. chief geophysicist).	• Recommend projects without the scrutiny of a competent technical audit.
• Recommend expenditures for projects based on team decisions.	• Approve expenditures without approval from appropriate functional managers.

AMT LEADER ROLE*

Objective: Coordinate the team's efforts to accomplish goals and objectives.

The AMT leader's chief responsibility is to coordinate and facilitate the activity of the team to ensure team focus and input from all disciplines.

The Leader is:	The Leader is not:
• A coordinator/facilitator	• A boss.
• An engineer/geoscientist who spends less than 15 percent of his time on administrative tasks dealing with the team.	• A full-time AMT manager/leader.
• Focusing the majority of his effort on technical work to accomplish team goals and objectives	• Allowing administrative tasks of the team to overshadow his technical responsibilities.

The Leader does:

- Coordinate the goal-setting process with the team and management.

- Call, chair, and document all formal team meetings and arrange for informal work sessions when appropriate.

- Actively seek input from all appropriate members and disciplines.

- Encourage new ideas and innovation from all disciplines.

- Strive to create an atmosphere of unity and cooperation.

- Arrange meetings and work sessions to maximize efficiency.

- Search out ideas from all members, especially new and young members.

- Lead effort to formalize team goals and objectives seeking input from ALL team members and from management.

The Leader does not:

- Determine the team's goals and objectives.

- Allow too many idle discussions, intradisciplinary discussions and wasted time in meetings.

- Look only for the obvious singular discipline input.

- Criticize or allow negative criticism to dominate discussions or reviews.

- Allow trivial arguments to continue.

- Expect attendance from all members at every meeting.

- Allow a few strong personalities to dominate the team.

- Wait for management deadline to gather team goals.

AMT "RESPONSIBLE MANAGER" ROLE*

Objective: Support the AMT leader and facilitate communication with management.

The Responsible Manager's chief responsibility is to support and develop the team leader to accomplish the team's goals and objectives. He is also to act as a liaison between the AMT and the management team.

The AMT Manager is:

- A coach/communicator

- A functional manager who spends less than 20 percent of his time on team administrative tasks.

- Mainly behind the scene in the AMT.

The AMT Manager is not:

- A boss.

- A full-time AMT manager.

- Focal point of team.

The AMT Manager does:

- Support and mentor the leader; provide guidance and opinion when needed.

- Give input on goals and objectives that are consistent with company/division objectives.

- Ensure that the proper mix of talent is maintained for the required job.

- Communicate personnel issues to functional managers (including input for salary administration and evaluations).

- Seek functional manager's input when needed.

- Is present at the majority of team meetings, especially when major decisions are being made.

- Communicate on a regular basis. (Leader notes database, memos, informal meetings).

- Promote new ideas and unique solutions.

- Hold members accountable for work product and timing.

- Conduct post operations reviews (i.e., post drill review, etc.)

- Allocate team members to only one team.

The AMT Manager does not:

- Manage or direct the team or the leader.

- Determine the team's goals and objectives.

- Enlist help from other AMTs on a regular basis.

- Deal with the personnel issues directly.

- Assume technical audit role for all disciplines.

- Let AMT struggle with decisions unproductively.

- Meet only once a week to discuss major items.

- Look for cookie cut solutions and procedures rather than being over-critical (negative) of new ideas.

- Conduct regular follow-up on work plans.

- Look back.

- Allow multiple team membership.

FUNCTIONAL MANAGER ROLE*

Objective: Responsible for technical quality of the final product in the functional area and functional operational support for all teams.

The functional manager's chief responsibility is to set technical standards and procedures to assure the high technical quality of projects performed by the teams. He is also responsible for administrative and operational activities required by his discipline to fully support the efforts of the teams.

The Functional Manager is:

- An auditor/trainer/staff developer.

- Primarily responsible for functional administrative, operational, and personnel matters.

- Mainly behind the scenes at the team level.

The Functional Manager does:

- Support and mentor the leader, provide guidance and opinion when needed.

- Give input on goals and objectives that are consistent with company/division objectives.

- Ensure that the proper mix of talent is maintained for the required job.

- Receive input on personnel issues from the AMT manager.

- Have a separate staff outside the AMTs to cover administrative and operational functions.

- Coordinate department goals with AMT goals and objectives.

The Functional Manager is not:

- A one-man show.

- A full-time AMT manager.

- Focal point of the team.

The Functional Manager does not:

- Manage or direct the team or the leader.

- Determine the team's goals and objectives.

- Enlist help from other AMTs on a regular basis.

- Deal with personnel issues independently.

- Require AMT members to spend large amounts of time on administrative functions not dealing directly with the AMT's goals.

- Have a separate agenda for AMT members.

*These charts are excerpted from a paper by John Girgis of Maxus Energy to be presented at the 1995 Indonesian Petroleum Association Meeting.

HOLDERBANK

Holderbank is another corporate example of successful transnational teamwork. It is a Swiss conglomerate composed of companies in 34 countries. The company produces and distributes ready-mixed concrete, cement, aggregates, and concrete chemicals. A variety of teams work throughout the organization including: working teams, productivity circles, quality circles, and energy circles. Each is organized within the same function area but is also cross-functional. Many of these teams consist of members from different cultures.[4]

The potential for collision occurs because of their cultural differences such as team members' attitude toward work, accountability, religion, and customs (e.g., not looking into the eyes of the person to whom you are speaking, which is a behavior resulting from inferiority structured by cultural experience in India and Saudi Arabia). Holderbank addresses cultural differences through training and education. Numerous training programs for its multinational project teams and managers have been developed. These programs consist of workshops in productivity and project circles, team moderation, team dynamics, and team development coaching. The company's *Team Dynamics* courses and workshops have clearly designed program elements that focus on cross-cultural exercises. These exercises help participants understand the cultural uniqueness of their team members' behavior. The exercises are structured so that members of one culture explain their customs and traditions to the group. This is followed by honest discussions about how other team members' cultures are different.

Holderbank has had many successful experiences using this approach but has also had failures. Dr. Willi Walser, vice president of corporate human resources, states, "Mobilizing teams from various countries and motivating them to achieve high performance and successful results requires my total commitment and sensitivity for the various cultures and persons involved."[5]

THE GLOBALWORK TEAM MODEL

Many books have been written on the subject of achieving corporate goals through effective teamwork. Much has also been written on the challenge to global corporations to synthesize team members from different cultures into collaborative teams. However, there has been little guidance on how to establish and manage team operations against the backdrop of many cultures.

Although some global corporations, such as Maxus Energy and Holderbank, have found creative GlobalSolutions for their corporations, the speed at which corporations must meet global expansion leaves precious little time to experiment with strategies created by other companies. What would be most helpful would be a model to guide corporations through the process of creating collaborative teams at all levels of the organization, wherever they are in their current team processes.

Figure 6-1 depicts a unique approach by proposing the creation of a culturally specialized team called the Cultural Process Team (CPT) to systematically move teams from collision to collaboration and keep them consistently operating at that level.

FIGURE 6-1

Model for Collaborative GlobalWork Teams

CULTURAL PROCESS TEAM

Experience in change management has shown that external consultants are effective facilitators of change and mediators of conflict because of their broad experience base and objectivity. Based on this time-tested concept, corporations can achieve similar results by establishing the Cultural Process Team (CPT) as an internal consulting team with responsibility for assisting organizational teams at all levels. The CPT would not only be responsible for helping teams with their internal team process, they would also facilitate the integration of teams corporatewide. Just as computers are linked through Local Area Networks (LANS), the threads of cultural influence on team processes must be linked throughout the organization.

Thus, the Cultural Process Team functions as a conduit for all cultural efforts within the organization. This team must deal with cultural impact on three intervention levels to facilitate the movement of teams from collision to coexistence and on to collaboration: proactive interventions during the early stages of team formation implemented to prevent—as much as possible—team cultural collisions before they occur (formational interventions); interventions as teams operate on a day-to-day basis to ensure that team and company operations remain on track and on schedule (operational interventions); and active interventions to move team members from collision back to collaboration when conflicts within the team arise (mediational interventions).

CPT INTERVENTIONS

Activities of the CPT at each level of intervention would depend upon the needs of the company and team members. However, there are basic activities common to team needs that can serve as a starting point for new CPTs. These activities would include, but not be limited to, the following:

(1)   ***Formational Interventions***
- Consult with Management in Configuration of Teams
- Conduct Individual Cultural Assessments and Give Feedback to Team Members
- Provide Cultural Awareness Training
- Set up Change Management Policies
- Recommend Team Member/Leader Selection Criteria
- Outline Team Process Factors

(2)   ***Operational Interventions***
- Provide Coaching for Managers and Team Leaders Regarding Cultural Issues (e.g., Recommend Reporting Process Procedures)
- Suggest Appropriate Evaluation Feedback Methods for Team Members and Leaders
- Provide Translators and Translation Services
- Adapt and Change Interventions Already in Place
- Provide Special Training Sessions as Needed
- Interface with Selected Professionals on Special Issues (e.g., legal and contract issues)

(3)   ***Mediational Interventions***
- Provide Conflict Resolution Services
- Arrange for Team Member/Leader Reassignment

CPT MEMBER COMPETENCIES

Members of the Cultural Process Team will need similar competencies as those discussed in Chapter 5:

- Communication Skills—listening, verbal, nonverbal, writing, and language
- Conceptual Process Skills—problem solving/decision making, negotiating, open-minded, innovative, perceptive, anticipating, and discerning
- Leadership Skills—tolerant, flexible, persuasive, consensus building, coaching, change-oriented, patient, interviewing, and bottom-line focused

- Project Management Skills—delegating, scheduling, forecasting, strategic planning, process focused, and prioritizing
- Technical Skills—computer, task and function specific

Additionally, CPT member skills should also include a basic understanding of the major national cultures represented in the company. Also helpful is knowledge of the laws and country parameters in which the team is working. Also, CPT members should be sensitive to national changes and crises that impact employees and resulting team processes. For example, currency fluctuations, government political shifts, natural disasters, wars, or terrorist attacks. Many of these events appear in the news media and affect the comfort level and working relationships of company teams.

Although it is critically important for Cultural Process Team members to have as many of these competencies as possible, no one individual can perform well in all of these skill areas. However, the Cultural Process Team should identify a pool of experts, either inside the company or external, who can provide specialized information and skills which complement competencies. Training for CPT members also is crucial to increase their skill levels. Companies who do not have qualified employees who can serve on this Cultural Process Team may want to use external consultants for some or all of the team member slots.

If CPT members will be chosen internally, it is recommended that one member from each major culture group be selected to serve on the CPT. For example, in the AOC Management Group discussed in Chapter 3, the team would be composed of one liaison from each of the major countries—Australia, Egypt, Norway, Finland, Great Britain, and India. This five-member CPT will assist other AOC Management Group teams in developing their teamwork process and in creating a company strategic intervention plan to pinpoint areas of potential problems. All CPT members have the responsibility to communicate the process as it is developed to their national groups, discuss any points that need to be adjusted, and promote buy-in for the entire worker population from that country.

This team process can be charted with a graphic that can be shared later with teams and team leaders. In this way the Cultural Process Team can map out its process to identify potential obstacles and barriers. The CPT will be an ongoing team and will meet on a regular basis to check how the strategy and process is working and to make corrections and additions as needed.

EXAMPLES OF FORMATIONAL INTERVENTIONS

CONDUCT INDIVIDUAL CULTURAL ASSESSMENTS

Most multinational teams experience collisions in working relationships and often do not realize that these conflicts come from the clash of cultural beliefs. Understanding individual cultures is the first step toward an effective GlobalWork team process. All team members need knowledge of their own individual values and workstyles in order to cooperate effectively with others on their team.

First, all employees should complete a cultural assessment survey. It is extremely important to emphasize that cultural concepts are neither good nor bad—they are just deeply ingrained beliefs within every human being. Employees need the assurance that all cultures are equal and that no specific culture has priority within the team process.

Early in the group process, the CPT facilitator should create an non-threatening atmosphere by assuring employees that their answers will not affect their jobs or their pay, that the results of their individual cultural assessment will be kept private and will not be shared with others. Following the survey, individual assessment profiles should be discussed with each team member in one-on-one interviews.

CONDUCT CULTURAL AWARENESS TRAINING

After all employees have discussed their individual profile analyses, the team members will meet to explore the effect their shared culture has on their individual behaviors and to explore how they may be similar to or different from individuals from the cultures of other team members. Cultural variables should be introduced in a team meeting with an explanation of how this knowledge can improve the teamwork process. This discussion should take place in the context of the issues surrounding the work project and its status because this provides a more comfortable environment in which to learn about cultural differences.

The group should focus first on their common ground—the cultural beliefs that are shared by all. To ensure that no inferences or finger-pointing behavior occurs, these sessions should be carefully managed by the facilitator. The goal of this effort is not to become academically correct in cultural knowledge but to better understand the cultural values that impact the workplace.

CONSULT WITH MANAGEMENT IN CONFIGURATION OF TEAMS

The Cultural Process Team should consult with management on the identification and formation of project teams. Assistance could be provided in areas such as the selection of team leaders and members, determining their responsibilities, and targeting possible areas of conflict. These project teams will be structured around the company's work projects. In the AOC example, the Cultural Process Team would make recommendations to management on the selection of teams for each phase of construction and project leaders for each of the teams based on cultural considerations.

Teams need boundaries within which to work. Contrary to popular belief, boundaries do not always result in inflexible team behavior. Appropriate boundaries are necessary for effective teamwork so team members will know what is expected of them. For example, meeting agendas with suggested time limits are helpful as are clear and explicit ground rules for team behavior. Team leaders should remember that all team members need time to adapt to team methods and processes as they continue to search for better ways of working together.

"The GRIP model," Mary O'Hara-Devereaux and Robert Johansen explain, "can be a collaborative space in which team members explore their views of goals (results needed to achieve purposes), relationships (building relationships, maintaining trust and good communications), information (available resources including money, technology, time), and processes (work procedures and training to complete tasks)."[6] Common understanding in these areas allows a team to get a GRIP on its work together at a high level. Goals can be represented in a graphic, focusing the team's attention forward from present activities. Procedures and processes can be illustrated as a process map, collaboratively developed by the team. Graphics can be instrumental in keeping the team aligned and on target even if team members work at different locations.

Technology, generally, can be helpful if used cautiously and supported with orientation and training that makes cultural biases explicit. Multinational corporations should develop guidelines for GlobalWork team start-ups and suggest best practices for technology use.

An example of productive multicultural teams is found at Owens-Corning. Composed of people from the Americas, Europe, and Asia, the teams' objective was to qualify all of the company's global sources of glass fiber to obtain a consistent quality that met its North American customers' demands. The goal was to adapt the American product to different manufacturing hardware that existed in other worldwide locations.[7] A key to the whole process was the team's ability to work closely with its customers to develop a clear understanding of their expectations. This understanding enabled Owens-Corning to reengineer a product that could be qualified and released to manufacturing in three and a half months instead of the nine to twelve months that it normally had been taking.

RECOMMEND TEAM LEADER SELECTION CRITERIA

As a proactive or formational intervention, the Cultural Process Team should assist management in the selection of team members and team leaders. To select team leaders, evaluate employees through group discussions, on-the-job observations, and individual cultural profiles. The objective is to choose leaders who can help create an environment in which work processes can be developed and negotiated. Leaders should be selected based on the competencies listed in Chapter 5 which include:

- Flexibility
- Willingness to support the process
- Desire to help the team work together
- Understanding of and appreciation for team cultural factors
- Ability to listen and communicate ideas
- Ability to focus on the origin of feelings that cause team member behaviors

Leaders of GlobalWork Teams should follow these strategic suggestions:

- Design a communications flow chart showing how information will be shared. Plan specific communication and translation procedures.
- Assign checkpoint responsibilities to ensure that team members understand and can act on the information they receive.
- Know when to use cultural translators to ensure clarity in the transfer of team information.
- Remember that specific job training may facilitate team communication and even transcend cultural variables. For example, a Swedish engineer may have a great deal in common with an engineer from the U.K. even though they are from different countries.
- Build trust and relationships to work toward a team objective.
- Develop teamwork processes based on cultural team mix.

Before team leaders meet with their project teams, they should have training in teambuilding and team management to develop knowledge and skill in how to conduct meetings, brainstorm, and problem solve. They should also meet with the CPT and discuss the teamwork process they will follow with their multicultural teams. Since they will be reporting the results of their teamwork to executive management, they also should schedule a meeting with the manager who will review the team's decisions.

Team leaders must move slowly in forming a team process culture. Team members may feel threatened if they believe they are being asked to give up their primary culture to participate.

EXAMPLES OF OPERATIONAL INTERVENTIONS

TRANSLATORS AND TRANSLATION SERVICES

Team leaders are much more effective if they are multilingual. If they are not fluent in team member languages, they should provide translators or interpreters for the team, preferably people who can translate both in writing and orally. The following list presents important ideas for working with translators/interpreters:

- Brief the translators/interpreters on the discussion topics or if there is a written presentation or outline, provide a copy and a glossary of terms beforehand and review them before the event.
- Speak slowly and group your sentences around single topics, avoiding slang and colloquial expressions.
- Use charts and other visuals where possible.
- Use metaphors and analogies only if you know they are commonly understood within the local culture. Avoid military terms as they are offensive to most cultures.
- Use specific, quantifiable terms whenever possible.
- Monitor the team members' facial expressions and other body language for signs of confusion or misunderstanding.
- Talk to team members, not the interpreter.[8]

Translators can also use graphics and write important points in the team members' languages. In team meetings with large numbers, the members can be grouped by their languages for translation. This is often done in conventions and conferences where translation equipment is not available. Also the use of networked computers in face-to-face meetings greatly improves team effectiveness—particularly when multiple languages can be used.[9]

Over the next decade, communication tools—from e-mail to group decision support systems—will be supported by computer-assisted translation services. Currently, the following are two tools that offer some assistance in translating:

- A group decision support system, Group Systems — Although this system is designed primarily for use in English, it has an editing function that allows menus and commands to be entered in other languages compatible with a keyboard. In the future, group decision support systems will have to address the issue of multiple languages and presentations for instructions as well as user participation.[10]

- AT&T Language Line — Important phone calls can be interpreted with the help of this tool.[11]

Every situation is different. What works for one team may not work for another. Brainstorming meetings are critical for problem solving—linking brains is as important as linking computers through Local Area Networks (LANs) or Wide Area Networks (WANs). Of course, linkages can occur face-to-face or the connection can be by:

- Telephone (audio)
- Satellite (video) conferencing
- Computer/fax: person-to-person
- Internet: multiple users

After leaders have discussed the teamwork process and the specific responsibilities with the team, they must match team members and tasks. They must be aware of the team members' competencies and determine if the team will have to add members or seek external resources to complete assignments. Individual interests must also be taken into account.

RECOMMEND REPORTING PROCESS PROCEDURES

Preparing project reports can often be difficult for multinational teams. Low-context Americans or Germans may take great pains to prepare a clear, detailed written report about everything involved. On the other hand, high-context Saudi Arabians or Brazilians may want to talk about the report informally and review a graphic that documents the highlights. To accommodate each member's cultural preference, the team should establish standard reporting formats in a way that blends cultural expectations so that no documentation preference rules by default. A mix of text and graphics would be a good starting point.[12] Although leaders may naturally prefer a solution compatible with their own culture, their challenge is to be effective with all the cultures.

INFLUENCE ON TEAM FUNCTIONS

All teams, regardless of level or function, work from two perspectives:

*   First, the abstract—defining a goal or task result
*   Then the concrete—implementing the plan

Intercultural teamwork in a corporate setting often has at least two other dimensions or layers of complexity in addition to its cultural factors. First, team members may find themselves working with other members from a variety of functions rather than only from the same profession. Second, teams sometimes span organizational boundaries and corporate cultures, such as in strategic alliances and joint ventures. So, a team member may be working with individuals from other cultures, other professional subcultures and sometimes other corporate cultures—all at once.

These teams must learn to work together to solve cross-functional problems and to attain cultural synergy. "We are finding more and more that it is not geniuses we need for success, but competent people who know how to work together, to seek solutions together. Team solutions are almost always better than individual ones," said Roland Berra of Hoffman LaRoche.[13]

With heightened complexity in the external business environment, companies will tend to rely more on cross-functional teams. Getting people from various professional subcultures even within the same country to work effectively together can be a challenge in itself. "It is not very difficult to create a team of engineers or a team of accountants, or even lawyers," said Theodore Papalexopoulos of Titan Cement. "But it is terribly difficult to create a team that works well with one lawyer, one engineer, one chemist and one accountant. Young managers do not know how to communicate sufficiently with people outside their own special field. It's as if one were speaking Chinese and the other French."[14] Papalexopoulos's strategy is to add into the team someone who is professionally bilingual—for example, an engineer with an MBA.

He points to excessive specialization at too early an age as the source of this communication problem and finds that team members who can build bridges between other individuals are valuable in moving the team forward.

When these teams are also transnational, team members must have competencies to deal with the obvious language issues as well as the cultural differences. Diverse cultural teams are subject to increased ambiguity, complexity, and confusion in decision making. Interaction becomes more difficult because team members see situations, understand them, and act upon them differently based on their cultural assumptions. However, at the same time, the creative potential of a transnational team is immense, and the competencies within such a group can be a critical organizational resource—for understanding new culturally diverse market segments and for developing unique solutions to difficult problems.[15]

In hiring workers or selecting team members, companies traditionally analyze task requirements and take the candidate who seems to be the best match for the outlined job requirements. Some corporations are beginning to develop a work model that begins with the employee. They assess his skills and place him in a position of strength. Instead of looking for one person who best fits the ability needed to perform a specific task, more than one worker with different skills may be needed to get the job done.

Most information on teamwork centers around teams located in an office environment (e.g., management, software development, marketing). Very little has been written about non-office type teams (e.g., construction, delivery services, oil rig maintenance).

Consider a road construction crew on the AOC project, for example. The entire construction project is divided into many steps or tasks, each of which will be completed by a different work crew.

- One crew is responsible for surveying the land.
- Another crew draws up the road blueprint.
- Still another uses heavy equipment to prepare the ground.
- One crew is responsible for hauling off the excess dirt.
- Another crew prepares the road surface material.
- A separate crew is responsible for surfacing the road.
- And still another paints lines on the finished surface or sets up signs on the side of the road.

Construction management does not try to hire a worker who can perform all of these steps well. They select workers who are qualified and have had previous experience with a specific phase of construction to work on a certain team or crew. Heavy equipment operators do not need the same competencies or skills as surveyors. Yet they must have the ability to see how their phase of work fits into the whole road construction process and how their performance can affect the successful completion of the project.

CULTURAL SYNERGY

Synergy results when team members collaborate—when they listen to each other and enter into the private worlds of their teammates. As Philip R. Harris and Robert T. Moran say, "[Synergy] can occur when diverse or disparate groups of people work together. The objective is to increase effectiveness by sharing perceptions, insights, and knowledge. The complexity and shrinking of today's world literally forces people to capitalize on their differences."[16] Team members have two choices:

- They can either try to impose *their way* upon the other team members, often to the mutual detriment of the team, or
- They can work together to form a kinetic team process culture.

The team's resources can be strengthened when intercultural differences are used for synergy rather than allowing them to become a cause for divisiveness. The differences of perception that arise from different cultural factors and national parameters, education and training backgrounds, and work experiences can enrich the GlobalWork team's ability to solve problems and accomplish project tasks. This synergy helps establish a strong team culture that enhances team communication and stimulates growth and collaboration. Collaboration should be evident not only within each GlobalWork team but also in the interaction between company teams within the corporation.

A GLOBALWORK TEAM MOTTO

Chapter 7

Never–Ending Transformation

Never-Ending Transformation

S ome industries, because of their basic products and markets, seem to have a history of never-ending transformation. The automobile makers are at the top of this list. They must constantly redesign their products, reengineer their systems, and attract their customers with new and innovative cars.

FORD MOTOR COMPANY

In January 1995, Alexander J. Trotman, Ford Motor Company's chairman, launched a sweeping remake of the world's number two auto maker. "The pressures driving Trotman to reshape Ford," says James B. Treece, "are painfully obvious: With completely independent auto units designing and selling their own vehicles on each side of the Atlantic, Ford has long paid a price in duplicated effort, waste, and high costs. Top-heavy and bureaucratic, Ford spends far too much time—and money—designing new cars."[1]

The first step in Trotman's Ford 2000 program is combining the North American and European units into a unified company. This process should transform Ford into a more efficient competitor as global product teams now design autos to be sold around the world. Trotman's vision amounts to a transformation of the 91-year-old company into the forefront of companies that are coordinating global operations. "In terms of global integration, this puts [Ford] among the leaders now," says George Yip, an associate professor at UCLA's Anderson Graduate School of Management.[2]

Yet combining the operations of these two independent units will be no easy task. As Morgan Stanley & Company analyst Scott F. Merlis explains, "Ford 2000, in a sense, is the largest merger in history. Ford of Europe and Ford North America together [are] a $94 billion company, and RJR-Nabisco was only $24 billion in revenues."[3] Like any merger, there are great risks involved:

- Asking European and American designers to take into account the needs of diverse markets may slow Ford's new-auto development process rather than speed it up.

- Vehicles designed to satisfy drivers around the world may end up pleasing no one.

A transformation of this scope posses huge management and morale challenges as vast numbers of workers will find themselves in new jobs with new bosses. Ford has created five new "Vehicle Centers"—four in the United States and one in Europe. Each center is responsible for designing a different type of vehicle worldwide. Approximately 500 Americans have moved to Europe to join the new European team overseeing small-car development and an equal number of Europeans have moved to Dearborn to design all of Ford's rear-wheel-drive cars and commercial trucks.

Trotman is also counting on a shift to these product-oriented teams to improve productivity. To ease the transition, managers from both sides of the Atlantic are also engaged in a massive reengineering project. Some 500 Ford employees from different countries spent nine months at Dearborn in 1994 examining and rewriting the manuals on every job they did. Ford's aim is to minimize cultural disputes over doing things "their way" versus "our way" and avoid as much as possible internal power struggles and team member conflicts.

One of Trotman's goals is to cut Ford's bureaucracy. He has instituted "no fault" meetings where managers can admit to problems knowing that the problem, not the message-bearer—will be attacked. "By eliminating 20% of top managers, instituting 'no fault' meetings, and creating multifunction teams to design and market cars," Treece continues, "Trotman is breaking Ford's once-rigid bureaucracy. New car projects are now O.K.'d in less than a month."[4]

"There absolutely is less bureaucracy," says Allan R. Kammer, the head of Ford' Escort vehicle line. "We are getting a lot of things done more quickly now."[5] He regularly finds cost savings by choosing the best methods from each organization. The U.S. system for coordinating the redesign of prototype parts was better, allowing parts to be redesigned faster and with less waste than in Europe. And Europe's practice of monitoring the engineering work that arises from warranty claims at the factory made more sense than the North American do-it-at-headquarters procedure.

But Ford 2000 does not stop here. In Trotman's judgment, the merger is moving smoothly. So much so that in 1996 South America and Asia will also join the European-American merger. And by decade's end, the global transformation could slash $3 billion from Ford's annual costs. These savings will come from eliminating the duplication of product development and turning to fewer, global suppliers for necessary parts.

Although the early signs are good, it will be several years before Ford 2000 can be evaluated. The first cars developed under Ford 2000 will not hit the showrooms until late 1997. However, if Ford can manage this corporate culture change and build effective cross-cultural teams, Ford 2000 should position this automaker for success in the 21st Century. With new ventures under way in China, Vietnam, India, and Poland, and a restructuring in South America, Trotman is counting on Ford's global approach to fuel sales in fast-growing emerging markets.

GLOBAL WORK TEAM RESOURCES

As corporations continue to assign projects to team members from different cultures and locations, more resources are needed to promote team collaboration. The development of these resources to assist with GlobalWork team issues is just beginning. GlobalWork team assessment instruments, films and videos, interactive training materials, games, and exercises are just appearing in the marketplace.

ASSESSMENTS

CLARKE CONSULTING GROUP

Clarke Consulting Group has designed several questionnaires that they use with clients in a coordinated research initiative including other ethnographic research methods as well. The questionnaires assist in developing quantitative and qualitative information about the goals, issues, and challenges facing companies in the global marketplace. The following four surveys can be administered to both headquarters and local subsidiary staff in both the native language and in English.

- **Global Teamwork Inventory** looks at the executive leadership team of the global company in nine areas:

    - vision and strategy
    - goal achievement
    - communication and information sharing
    - decision making
    - team member relations
    - cultural synergy
    - meeting productivity
    - leadership

- **International Management Survey** identifies cross-cultural stress points of international management behavior in the following nine areas:

    - planning
    - organizing
    - leading

- decision making
- motivating
- evaluating
- training
- conflict resolution
- negotiating

- **Intercultural Competency Inventory** develops a *competency* profile of both headquarters and local subsidiary staff in 10 core intercultural style and skill areas:

  - general intercultural skills
  - cross-cultural adaptability
  - listening
  - relationship building
  - giving and receiving feedback
  - persuasion
  - problem solving
  - negotiation
  - meeting productivity
  - use of communication media

- **Transnational Climate Survey** takes the *temperature* of an organization by determining the degree to which people's expectations about working in the organization are met. Some of the climate dimensions that are assessed include:

  - work goals
  - results motivation
  - morale
  - performance evaluation and rewards
  - decision-making
  - communication
  - cross-cultural management
  - training and development
  - workplace relations
  - organization change

SRI

SRI is a consulting firm that offers selection consulting. Its organizational services focus on two important related areas:

international personnel assessment and organizational planning and management development. These services include auditing the corporate international human resources function, analyzing organization and management needs, and developing tailored action plans for organization development, research, and planning. For organizations, SRI offers:

- **Global Manpower Integration**—integrating domestic high-potential management programs with international staffing needs and creating leadership data pools of foreign national managers in world areas.

- **Assessing individual employees** in relation to specific organizational needs and international projects, including human resources planing, career development, and succession planning.

- **Assessing the International Training Candidate and Spouse** providing:

  Pre-Evaluation.
  – Needs Analysis
  – Reference Interview
  – Overview and Questionnaire
  – Briefing

  Evaluation Procedures.
  – Background Information Form
  – Testing
  – Interviews
  – Cross-Cultural Videotapes
  – Joint Couple Interview and Wrap-Up
  – Focused Adaptability and Behavioral Assessment Report
  – Confidentiality
  SRI's Candidate Profile
  SRI's Employee Summary Profile

INTERCULTURAL MANAGEMENT PUBLISHERS

Cross Cultural Management–Your Personal Follow-up is an interactive computer program for personal insight offered by Intercultural Management Publishers which is based in The

Netherlands. This unique, interactive program is a personal follow-up to their Cross Cultural Management video. Using the criteria which have been identified in the video, it helps individuals understand how their personal profile affects the way they think about others and gives them the tools for better understanding and communication. The program generates a helpful list of personal recommendations on doing business within other cultures and makes a comparison between the individual's profile and that of the average compatriot and the average inhabitants of the great economic world powers.

VIDEOS

There are a number of videos available for use in studying the cultures of various nationalities. These films are especially helpful in team training sessions. A description of the video is given with an address of the company.

Doing Business in Mexico is a video training program to advise and educate viewers on doing business in Mexico. With insights into the Mexican culture, the video provides information on how to:

- *Make the right contacts to assure business success*
- *Build solid, long-term business relationships*
- *Make sure work is done right, done on time*
- *Communicate: understand what your host is really saying*
- *Use proper etiquette that wins friends in Mexico*
- *Negotiate effectively within the "Mexican timetable"*
- *Feel more at ease in Mexico, enjoy yourself more*

This 30-minute video comes with a complete study guide to maximize the benefits received. Produced and distributed by:

Big World Inc.
1350 Pine Street, Suite 5
Bolder, CO 80302
(800) 682-1261

The Multicultural Customer is a new video program from
Salenger Films that is designed to help employees provide effective
customer service (face-to-face and on the telephone) to external
multicultural customers. This 20 minute video emphasizes these
basic interpersonal skills:

- *Sensitivity*
- *Patience*
- *Flexibility*
- *Spending extra time with customers when needed*

This program also offers techniques to help when talking with
customers who have a heavy accent or who may not be fluent in
your language. This video helps develop the interpersonal skills
necessary to satisfy the expectations of all multicultural customers.
Leader's Guide included.

Produced and distributed by:

> Salenger Films
> 1635 12th Street
> Santa Monica, CA 90404
> (310) 450-1300

New Skills For Global Management is a video on globalization.
Global management is not confined to a few people at the top of an
organization. Globalization affects everyone in an organization—
from domestic line supervisors to global product managers. In this
35-minute video, Stephen Rhinesmith addresses managers
regarding the new skills and mindsets required for effective
management:

- *Managing Global Competitiveness*
- *Managing Complexity and Conflict*
- *Managing Multicultural Teams*
- *Managing Adaptability*

This video is accompanied by a leader's guide with instruction notes, exercises, and overhead masters and an audio cassette.

Doing Business Internationally—The Cross-Cultural Challenges is a video training package designed to enable managers to develop the skills and attitudes required for effective international management and to provide an in-depth analysis of the impact of culture on business practices. Combining graphics, live action, and interviews with international management consultant Stephen Rhinesmith and executives from Colgate-Palmolive, Ernst & Young, and AT&T, the video covers:

- *Internationalization*
- *What is Culture?*
- *Culture and International Negotiation*
- *Culture and International Management*
- *Culture and International Marketing*
- *Conclusion—The International Manager*

The 43-minute video is accompanied by a leader's guide, participant's workbook, and an audio cassette.

The Challenges of The North American Free Trade Agreement is a video presentation featuring Dean Allen Foster, director of Berlitz Cross Cultural Consulting. With information about the emerging NAFTA market—a partnership between the United States, Mexico, and Canada, key issues covered are:

- *The central principles of NAFTA*
- *Opportunities and threats to business*
- *Overview of the business, political and social climates in Mexico and Canada*
- *The cross-cultural skills needed to work successfully with Mexican and Canadian business colleagues.*

This 25-minute video is divided into four segments. Each segment may be shown separately for group discussion. The package also includes a leader's guide with instruction notes, additional information sources, a video transcript, and audio cassette.

Shedding Light on the European Single Market is a video package designed to provide managers with an in-depth analysis of key business and regulatory issues in the European Single Market, and the success factors for operating in Europe. It is divided into five parts:

- *Overview of the Single Market*
- *Financial issues*
- *Legal issues*
- *External trade*
- *Strategies*

The 45-minute video is updated for 1995 and is accompanied by a facilitator's support material booklet.

Produced and distributed by:

> MultiMedia Inc.
> 15 North Summit Street
> Tenafly, NJ 07670
> (800) 682-1992

Going International is a film series that consists of four films that help orient Americans to culture differences around the world:

- *Bridging The Culture Gap*
- *Managing The Overseas Assignment*
- *Beyond Culture Shock*
- *Welcome Home Stranger*

Films for non-U.S. citizens:
- – *Working In The USA*
- – *Living In The USA*

Film for all travelers:
- – *Going International - Safely*

Each film title has a user's guide for participants that expands upon the film/video and provides exercises, checklists, and additional resources. Produced and distributed by:

Griggs Productions
302 23rd Avenue
San Francisco, CA 94121
(415) 668-4200

BOOKS

Intercultural Press is a publisher of global and multicultural books.

Intercultural Press, Inc.
P O Box 700
Yarmouth, ME 04096
(207) 846-5168

Irwin Professional Publishing has a series of books on international topics.

Irwin Professional Publishing
1333 Burr Ridge Parkway
Burr Ridge, IL 60521-6489
(708) 789-4000

GAMES

The Global Diversity Game is a board game that provides a lively introduction to the trends and issues making up the challenges that businesses face in today's global economy. It is an instructional tool for global management development programs and an effective icebreaker for international management meetings.

The game is played by teams answering insightful and startling multiple-choice questions about Demographics, Jobs, Legislation and Society. Each question relates to the global business environment. Test questions focus on key workplace issues such as communication, motivation, reward and recognition, respect and trust.

Quality Educational Development, Inc.
41 Central Park West
New York, NY 10023
(214) 724-3335

Barnga is a card game in which differences among cultures are simulated by different versions of the game rules. Difficulties are magnified by the fact that players may not speak to each other, but can only communicate through gestures or pictures.

This game demonstrates that unless we recognize and respect the different assumptions underlying our interactions, we run into interpersonal conflict.

- As few as nine players or more can play.
- The play and debriefing can take as little as 45 minutes.
- It provides participants with enough material for an extended debriefing.
- The rules are few and simple. Participants can start playing within minutes.
- Participant instructions are provided in French and Spanish as well as English.
- It lends itself easily to effective experimentation.

Ecotonos is a tool for engaging in problem solving and decision making in multicultural groups. Methods and processes of decision making in these groups are analyzed, diagrammed, and compared, and guidelines for effectiveness are generated. Ecotonos requires at least three hours and at least three facilitators to work with small groups during the simulation for maximum value to be derived. It is most effective with no more than 50 and at least 12 participants.

The simulation package includes:

- Three sets of culture name buttons
- Ten sets of color-coded cultural rule cards
- Case studies

- Facilitator's manual for conducting the simulation
- Sample of decision-making process maps

> Intercultural Press, Inc.
> P O Box 700
> Yarmouth, ME 04096
> (207) 846-5168

As GlobalWork teams use these and other resources, they continue to define and redefine their work. By taking the steps as outlined in Figure 7-1—visionary leadership, innovative strategies, synthesis of cultures, integration of teams, ongoing flexibility, and never-ending transformation—multinational corporations and GlobalWork teams can successfully adapt to the Age of Transformation.

FIGURE 7-1

GlobalSolutions

V isionary Leadership
I nnovative Strategies
S ynthesis of Cultures
I ntegration of Teams
O ngoing Flexibility
N ever-Ending Transformation

TRANSFERRING THE GLOBAL WORK TEAM PROCESS

The same models and guidelines that work with multicultural teams are also effective for other types of company teams. Just as diverse cultural factors and national parameters affect the interaction of transnational teams, potential conflicts in different types of cultures and workstyles affect teamwork—for example, the differences between academic and business cultures, hearing professors and deaf students, technical and nontechnical workers. Most teams even from the same culture or profession jump into teamwork with no thought to the team process. Self-directed, cross-functional, and other types of teams should also begin with an assessment of each individual, develop cultural awareness and acceptance of all team members involved, and work together through negotiation to an acceptable plan of action.

ETHICS AND CULTURE

Do corporate executives think ethics matter? The Conference Board, a New York-based association of major corporations, says yes.[5]

According to "Corporate Ethics Practices," the 1992 survey of 1,900 corporations (with 264 companies responding) in the United States, Canada, Mexico, and Europe, they found that:

- **Codes are most common in the United States**. Some 84 percent of U.S. respondents have corporate ethics codes, while only 58 percent of non-U.S. firms have them. A parallel study by the Institute of Business Ethics in London found that 71 percent of its sample of United Kingdom companies had codes of ethics in 1991—up from 55 percent in 1987.

- **Chief executive officers are commenting "openly and often" on business ethics**. Among respondents in the United States, 31 percent of CEOs spoke out on ethics in the prior year; in Europe, traditionally more reticent on the subject, the figure was a surprisingly high 40 percent.

- **Ethics is increasingly popular in corporations**. Nearly half (45 percent) of the respondents' codes of ethics had been enacted since an earlier Conference Board survey in 1987. Financial firms, however, are still much less likely (57 percent) to have codes than companies in other industries (82 percent).

- **America and Europe have different views on codes**. In the United States, where codes tend to be seen as legal documents, the corporate legal counsel is often central to the drafting process. In Europe, where the code is more often viewed as a social compact between the company and its workers, boards of directors play a central role—and are far more apt to bring employee representatives into the drafting process.

- **Ethics training is on the rise**. Some 25 percent of the respondents have set up new ethics training programs, ethics committees, or ombudsman's offices in the last three years.[6]

The Conference Board cites four major reasons for these practices:

- **Global management issues**. Companies operating internationally "want to determine their company's 'core' values while simultaneously showing respect for local customs and practices."

- **Total quality management**. TQM, which typically requires workers "a core of shared commitments and values to develop and to achieve a high standard of production," depends on ethics for its success.

- **Workforce diversity**. Corporations are concerned about minority representation. In addition, they find that in an era of downsizing, "new and less experienced workers and managers are now responsible for decisions"—and need an ethical handle on decision-making.

- **Inadequate education and training**. In addition to deficiencies in science, math, and literacy, graduates of public secondary education lack ethical literacy.[7]

Although business ethics vary from country to country, today multiculturalism is one of the factors promoting a trend toward more ethical behavior.

MCDONNELL-DOUGLAS CODE OF ETHICS

Typical of many corporate codes, is the McDonnell-Douglas Code of Ethics. It contains nine bullet points that require employees to be:

- Honest and trustworthy in all our relationships;
- Reliable in carrying out assignments and responsibilities;
- Truthful and accurate in what we say and write;
- Cooperative and constructive in all work undertaken;
- Fair and considerate in our treatment of fellow employees, customers, and all other persons;
- Law abiding in all our activities;
- Committed to accomplishing all tasks in a superior way;
- Economical in utilizing company resources;
- Dedicated in service to our company and to improvement of the quality of life in the world in which we live.[8]

THE MINNESOTA PRINCIPLES

In 1992 the Minnesota Center for Corporate Responsibility created a guide to international business activities. The Minnesota Principles sets forth, four core moral values:

Proposition #1: Business activities must be characterized by fairness. We understand fairness to include equitable treatment and equality of opportunity for all participants in the marketplace.

Proposition #2: Business activities must be characterized by honesty. We understand honesty to include candor, truthfulness and promise-keeping.

Proposition #3: Business activities must be characterized by respect for human dignity. We understand this to mean that business activities should show a special concern for the less powerful and the disadvantaged.

Proposition #4: Business activities must be characterized by respect for the environment. We understand this to mean that business activities should promote sustainable development and prevent environmental degradation and waste of resources.[9]

In Rushworth Kidder's book, *How Good People Make Tough Choices*, he tells of the experience of Johnson & Johnson's Tylenol case in 1982 as an example of how a code of ethics can be effective.

> In the now-famous Tylenol tampering case in 1982 is an example of how a code of ethics can be effective. Executives at Johnson & Johnson received a chilling report: Several poisonings had been reported in the Chicago area, linked to Tylenol capsules laced with cyanide. Within the first twenty-four hours, two things were clear: There was a need for prompt action to prevent further poisonings, and there was no obvious way to determine whether the capsules had been adulterated by a disgruntled employee, contaminated by a flaw in the manufacturing process, or subjected to tampering after the product had been shipped. Also clear was the context: Tylenol producted $100 million annually for Johnson & Johnson, a company that, under the leadership of chairman James Burke, had recently revitalized its long-standing Credo, or code of ethics, through a series of meetings with executives.
>
> J & J's action was swift, extensive, and highly visible. In a sweeping recall, it removed all forms of Tylenol—not just the capsules—from every shelf in every store. Then, through a well-orchestrated campaign to inform the public of its concern for safety and through various incentives to attract customers, it reintroduced the now-tamper-proof product. Within eighteen months, it had regained its market share.[10]

Harvard Business School professor Laura L. Nash cites this case as one involving a corporate leadership style that puts ethics ahead of marketing. "Having personally interviewed the three top officers involved," she writes, "I am certain that no textbook marketing analysis could quantify or even identify the factors that informed their strategy."[11]

> *From an economic and public relations standpoint, one could have made a very reasonable argument for keeping the product on the shelves:* The contamination was not the company's fault, and did not appear to have originated from a J & J facility: this was an isolated incident, the result of aberrant behavior, the benefits of the product to the majority of the public vastly outweighed the injuries that might occur if the product remained on the shelves.[12]

Nash further notes that the more than two hundred decisions had to be made within the first twenty-four hours. What held those decisions on an ethical track, apparently, was the firm's Credo. This page-long statement has four parts—arranged in what J & J employees understand to be priority order—covering the company's responsibility to customers, to employees, to communities, and finally to stockholders. It begins, "We believe our first responsibility is to the doctors, nurses and patients, to mothers and fathers and all others who use our product and services."[13]

Unlike some corporate codes that hang numbly on walls or circulate to impress the public, this one had been kept alive—so much so that, when the time came for rapid fire decision-making up and down the corporate ladder, there was little need to ask "What's the company line?" or "Should we stonewall this one?" The Credo, and the commitment of the chairman to its implementation, was understood to be the standard. While stockholders' profit mattered, public safety mattered more. "As one manager later told me," Professor Nash writes, "'Tylenol was the tangible proof of what top management had said at the Credo challenge meetings. You came away saying, "My God! You're right. We really do believe this. It's for real. *And we did what was right.*"[14]

STRATEGIES FOR THE FUTURE

Gary Hamel, a management professor at the London Business School believes corporations have spent too much time looking at benchmarking competitors. "I believe benchmarking is a good discipline, but I do not want only to be concerned about the current best practice. I want to think about the next practice. If you're duplicating what somebody is already doing very well, you get to be on par, at best. You never lead," he states.[15]

Today many of tomorrow's mega-opportunities are just being conceived and born. Alliances are being formed, competencies assembled, and experiments conducted. Those companies with a view of where they want to go and who can assemble and orchestrate resources across the globe have a chance for handsome rewards.

Look at Motorola. It envisions a world in which people, not places, will have phone numbers; where hand-held devices will link people anywhere; and where such devices can deliver text and video along with sound. To create this world, Motorola will have to strengthen its competencies in digital compression, flat-screen displays, and battery technology. In addition, it will have to increase the presence of its brand in the minds of global consumers.[16]

Unlike vision, which connotes a dream, foresight is based on deep insights into technology trends, demographics, regulation, and lifestyle, and how these can be harnessed to rewrite the rules and create new competitive space.

DEVELOPING FORESIGHT

Few management teams spend as much time managing opportunities as they do managing operations. To gain foresight the corporation should not be viewed as a collection of business units. "Think of it as a collection of competencies . . . These are competence-based opportunities that reside between or around existing products," Gary Hamel proposes. "As much as anything, foresight comes from wanting to make a real difference in people's lives."[17]   Sony's Akio Morita says, "Our plan is to lead the public with new products rather than ask them what kind of products they want. The public does not know what is possible, but we do."[18]

To get to the future first, the transnational company needs the emotional and intellectual energy of every team member. Most important, the company must today look at what it is doing *right now* to intercept the future—what competencies team members must be developing now, what customers it needs to understand now, and what distribution channels it needs to explore now to create the future.

CREATING TOMORROW

In *Change Management: A Model For Effective Organization Performance,* authors Patricia K. Felkins, B. J. Chakiris, and Kenneth N. Chakiris show how to coordinate corporate energy and resources to bring about integrated change. They present a practical, competency-based model that illustrates how change can be continuously facilitated through teamwork, collaborative data collection and analysis, and action planning and use an analytical process—Action Research Teaming—as a change strategy to bring about corporatewide participation, commitment, and learning for effective action and results.[19] In today's chaotic business environment, the effects of continuous change are everywhere—transforming the way companies define themselves, how they respond to customers, and how they will do business in the future. Only by effectively managing change can executives, managers, team leaders, human resource personnel, consultants, and other business professionals release the true potential of their corporation and encourage teams at all levels to work together to improve quality, productivity, and service.

GLOBALWORK TEAMS

GlobalWork teams must be working now to create tomorrow. For those corporations willing to make the commitment to create the future through visionary leadership, integrated strategies, synthesis of cultures, integration of teams, ongoing flexibility, and never-ending transformation, the rewards—and satisfaction—can be great.

Notes

Introduction

1. Dave Savona, "Can Foreigners Save L.A. Gear?" *International Business,* December 1994.
2. Ibid.
3. Douglas Harbrecht, Geri Smith, and Gail DeGeorge, "Ripping Down Walls Across the Americas," *Business Week,* December 26, 1994.
4. Ibid.
5. Nilly Landau, "Face to Face Marketing is Best," *International Business,* June 1994.
6. Edward M. Mervosh, Editorial, *International Business,* July 1994.
7. Bill Saporito, "The Eclipse of Mars," *Fortune,* November 28, 1994.
8. Associated Press, "Flagging a problem," *The Dallas Morning News,* June 8, 1994.
9. Edward M. Mervosh, "Boss's Bold New Boss," *International Business,* December 1994.
10. Ibid.
11. Lori Ioannou, "Stateless Executives," *International Business,* February 1995.
12. Lee Smith, "Stamina: Who Has it, Why You Need it, How You Get it," *Fortune,* November 28, 1994.
13. Ibid.
14. David Greising, "Globe Trotter: If it's 5:30, this must be Tel Aviv," *Business Week,* October 17, 1994.
15. Jay Mathews, "In search of profits...shares in Tom Peter's 'Excellence' companies fail to match S&P 500," *The Dallas Morning News,* November 21, 1994.
16. Gregory L. Miles, "Managing Explosive Foreign Growth," *International Business,* June 1994.
17. Ibid.
18. Ibid.
19. Ibid.
20. Ibid.
21. Ibid.

Chapter 1

1. Gregory L. Miles, "Marriages of Convenience," *International Business,* January 1995.
2. Stratford Sherman, "Andy Grove: How Intel Makes Spending Pay Off," *Fortune,* February 22, 1993.
3. Keith H. Hammonds, Kevin Kelly, and Karen Thurston, "The New World of Work," *Business Week,* October 17, 1994.
4. Ibid.
5. Betsy Simnacher, "Donations help schools keep up with computers," *The Dallas Morning News,* January 17, 1995.
6. Ibid.
7. "1992 Contributions Report," Pfizer Inc. and The Pfizer Foundation, Inc.
8. "Social Responsibility In Action Worldwide," Johnson & Johnson.
9. Ibid.
10. Thomas A. Stewart, "How To Lead A Revolution," *Fortune,* November 28, 1994.
11. Ibid.
12. Dave Savona, "Changing the Rules," *International Business,* January 1993.
13. Ibid.
14. Gregory L. Miles, "Multinational Future Shock, *International Business,* December 1994.
15. Ibid.

Chapter 2

1. Terence E. Deal and Allen A. Kennedy, *Corporate Cultures: The Rites and Rituals of Corporate Life,* Reading, MA: Addison-Wesley, 1982.
2. Noel M. Tichy and Stratford Sherman, *Control Your Destiny or Someone Else Will,* New York: HarperBusiness, 1993.
3. Ibid.
4. Gregory L. Miles, "The Trials of Two Acquirers," *International Business,* February, 1995.
5. Anne B. Fisher, "How to Make a Merger Work, *Fortune,* January 24, 1994.
6. Ibid.
7. Gregory L. Miles, "The Trials of Two Acquirers."
8. Ibid.
9. Ibid.
10. Ibid.
11. Ibid.
12. Ibid.
13. Ibid.
14. Ibid.

15. Ibid.
16. Stephen Silha, "The Future Isn't What It Used To Be," *Creative Living,* Winter 1993.
17. W. Mathew Juechter, "What it Really Takes to Transform a Company," ARC International, Ltd., 1993.
18. Gregory L. Miles, book review of *Competing for the Future. International Business*, July 1994.
19. Gary Hamel and C. K. Prahalad, *Competing for the Future*, Boston: Harvard Business School Press, 1994.
20. Ibid.
21. Ibid.
22. "Why Most Executives Never Make It To The Top," advertisement for CSX Intermodal, *International Business,* January 1995.
23. Mary O'Hara-Devereaux and Robert Johansen, *GlobalWork: Bridging Distance, Culture, & Time,* San Francisco: Jossey-Bass, 1994.
24. Ibid.
25. Nicola Phillips, *From Vision To Beyond Teamwork,* Burr Ridge, IL: Richard D. Irwin, Inc., 1995.
26. Daryl R. Conner, *Managing at the Speed of Change,* New York: Villard Books, 1992.
27. Margaret J. Wheatley, *Leadership and the New Science*, San Francisco: Berrett-Koehler, 1994.
28. W. Mathew Juechter, "What it Really Takes to Transform a Company."
29. Elizabeth J. Hawk, "Culture and Rewards," *Personnel Journal,* April 1995.
30. Ibid.
31. Ibid.
32. James C. Collins and Jerry I. Porras, *Built To Last,* New York: HarperBusiness, 1994.
33. Gene Calvert, *Highwire Management*, San Francisco: Jossey-Bass, 1993.

Chapter 3

1 "Industry Report," *Training,* October 1994.
2. Suzann D. Silverman, "Reporting in Tongues,"*International Business,* November 1994.
3. Ibid.
4. Niklaus Leuenberger, "The Fundamentals Never Change," *Profit Magazine,* September/October 1994.
5. Mary O'Hara-Devereaux and Robert Johansen, *GlobalWork: Bridging Distance, Culture & Time,* San Francisco: Jossey-Bass, 1994.
6. Farid Elashmawi, "Multicultural Management: A Key for the Success of Indonesian Petroleum Joint Ventures," Proceedings Indonesian Petroleum Association, 23rd Annual Convention, October 1994.

7. Ibid.
8. Ibid.

Chapter 4

1. Alan Richter and Cynthia Barnum, "When Values Clash," *HR Magazine,* September 1994.
2. Mary Mitchell, ""Managing Multicultural Project Teams Within The European Union," American Graduate School of International Management (Thunderbird) research paper, December 7, 1994.
3. Maud Tixier, "Management Styles Across Western European Cultures," *The International Executive,* July/August 1994.
4. Ibid.
5. Geert Hofstede, *Culture's Consequences: International Differences in Work-Related Values,* Beverly Hills: Sage, 1984.
6. David A. Victor, *International Business Communication,* HarperCollins, 1992.
7. Maud Tixier, "Management Styles Across Western European Cultures."
8. Charles Hampden-Turner and Alfons Trompenaars, *The Seven Cultures of Capitalism,* New York: Doubleday, 1993.
9. Ibid.
10. Mary O'Hara-Devereaux and Robert Johansen, *GlobalWork: Bridging Distance, Culture & Time,* San Francisco: Jossey-Bass, 1994.
11. Lee Gardenswartz and Anita Rowe, "Elements of Culture Impact Teamwork," International HR/Supplement, *HR News,* January 1995.
12. Ibid.
13. Mary O'Hara-Devereaux and Robert Johansen, *GlobalWork.*
14. Edward T. Hall, *Beyond Culture,* New York: Doubleday Anchor Books, 1976, and Geert Hofstede, *Culture's Consequences: International Differences in Work-Related Values.*
15. A. Furnham and S. Bochner, *Culture Shock: Psychological Reactions to Unfamiliar,* London: Methuen, 1986.
16. Helen Bloom, Roland Calori, and Philippe de Woot, *Euromanagement: A NewStyle for the Global Market,* London: Kogan Page Limited, 1994.
17. Tixier, "Management Styles Across Western European Cultures."
18. Zachary R. Townsend, "Leadership in France," American Graduate School of International Management (Thunderbird) research paper, May 13, 1994.
19. Ibid.
20. Mary O'Hara-Devereaux and Robert Johansen, *GlobalWork.*
21. Lee Gardenswartz and Anita Rowe, "Elements of Culture Impact Teamwork."
22. Ibid.
23. Charles Hampden-Turner and Alfons Trompenaars, *The Seven Cultures of Capitalism.*

24. Fons Trompenaars, *Riding the Waves of Culture*, Burr Ridge, IL: Irwin Professional Publishing, 1994.
25. Charles Hampden-Turner and Alfons Trompenaars, *The Seven Cultures of Capitalism.*
26. Geert Hofstede, *Culture's Consequences: International Differences in Work-Related Values.*
27. Ibid.
28. Interview with Bill Johnson at Texas Instruments in Dallas, Texas, February 1995.
29. Tixier, "Management Styles Across Western European Cultures."
30. Alan Goldstein, "A Team Player," *The Dallas Mornng News,* March 28, 1995.
31. Ibid.
32. Tixier, "Management Styles Across Western European Cultures."
33. Interview with Serge Ogranovitch, Center for Intercultural Training and Education.
34. Ibid.
35. Judith A. Starkey, "Diversity: An Accelerating Workforce Reality," *The Illinois Manufacturer*, May/June 1994.
36. Christopher A. Bartlett and Sumantra Ghoshal, *Managing Across Borders—The Transnational Solution,* Boston: Harvard Business School Press, 1989.
37. John R. Fulkerson, vice president organization and management development, "Managing Worldwide Diversity," presentation at the 18th Annual Conference of the Institute for International Human Resources, April 3, 1995 in Boston, Massachusetts.
38. Ibid.
39. Ibid.
40. Ibid.
41. Floria A. Maljers, "Inside Unilever: The Evolving Transnational Company," *The Harvard Business Review*, September–October, 1992.
42. Charles Hampden-Turner and Alfons Trompenaars, *The Seven Cultures of Capitalism.*

Chapter 5

1. Patrick Canavan, Corporate vice president and Motorola director of global leadership and organizational development, "Characteristics of the Global Leader," presentation at the 18th Annual Conference of the Institute for International Human Resources, April 4, 1995 in Boston, Massachusetts.
2. Ibid.
3. Philip R. Harris and Robert T. Moran, *Managing Cultural Differences,* 2nd ed., Gulf Publishing, 1989.

4. C. K. Prahalad, "Developing Core Competencies," presentation at the 18th Annual Conference of the Institute for International Human Resources, April 2, 1995 in Boston, Massachusetts.
5. Michael B. Goodman, *Working in a Global Environment: Understanding, Communicating, and Managing Transnationally,* Piscataway, NJ:IEEE, 1995.
6. Ibid
7. Nicola Phillips, *From Vision To Beyond Teamwork: 10 Ways to Wake Up And Shake Up Your Company,* Burr Ridge, IL: Irwin Professional Publishing, 1995.
8. Gary Hamel and C. K. Prahalad, *Competing for the Future: Breakthrough Strategies for Seizing Control of Your Industry and Creating the Markets of Tomorrow,* Boston: *Harvard Business School Press,* 1994.
9. Ibid.
10. Michael Marquardt and Angus Reynolds, *The Global Learning Organization,* Irwin, 1994.
11. Reyer (Rick) A. Swaak, "Global Competition Changes Old Habits And Thinking, International HR/Supplement to *HR News,* January 1995.
12. Ibid.
13. Peter Senge, *The Fifth Discipline,* New York: Doubleday, 1990.
14. Marcia Atkinson, "Build Learning into Work," *HR Magazine,* September 1994.
15. Mary O'Hara-Devereaux and Robert Johansen, *GlobalWork: Briding Distance, Culture & Time,* San Francisco: Jossey-Bass, 1994.
16. Peter Senge, *The Fifth Discipline.*
17. Marcia Atkinson, "Building Learning into Work."
18. Ibid.
19. Keith H. Hammonds, "The New World of Work," *Business Week,* October 17, 1994.
20. Ibid.
21. Mary Mitchell, "Managing Multicultural Project Teams Within The European Union," American Graduate School of International Management (Thunderbird) research paper, December 7, 1994.

Chapter 6

1. Interviews with Steve Ginsburgh, manager-organization services and employee development, Maxus Energy in Dallas and John Girgis, Senior manager-development, Maxus SES in Jakarta, Indonesia, 1995.
2. Ibid.
3. Ibid.
4. Interview with Dr. Willi Walser, vice president-corporate human resources of Holderbank in Holderbank, Switzerland, 1995.
5. Ibid.

6. Mary O'Hara-Devereaux and Robert Johansen, *GlobalWork: Bridging Distance, Culture & Time,* San Francisco: Jossey-Bass, 1994.
7. D. Keith Denton, "Process Mapping Trims Cycle Time," *HR Magazine,* February 1995.
8. Gary M. Wederspahn, "Working With Interpreters," *Cultural Diversity at Work,* November 1991.
9. P. Gray, L. Olfman, and H. Park, "The Interface Problem in International Group DDS," paper presented for the task force on International Group Decision Support Systems at the 21st Hawaii International Conference in Systems Sciences, Honolulu, January 5-7, 1988.
10. Ibid.
11. Ibid.
12. Helen Bloom, Roland Calori, and Philippe de Woot, *Euromanagemet; A New Style for the Global Market,* London: Kogan Page Limited, 1994.
13. Ibid.
14. Ibid.
15. Nicola Phillips, *From Vision To Beyond Teamwork: 10 Ways To Wake Up And Shake Up Your Company,* Burr Ridge, Il: Irwin Professional Publishing, 1995.
16. Robert T. Moran, "Making Globalization Work," *World Executive's Digest,* January 1993.

Chapter 7

1. James B. Treece, "Ford: Alex Trotman's daring global strategy," *Business Week,* April 3, 1995.
2. Ibid.
3. Ibid.
4. Ibid.
5. Ibid.
6. Rushworth Kidder, *How Good People Make Tough Choices,* William Morrow, 1995.
7. Ibid.
8. Ibid.
9. Ibid.
10. Ibid.
11. Ibid.
12. Ibid.
13. Ibid.
14. Ibid.
15. Gary Hamel and C. K. Prahalad, *Competing for the Future: Breakthrough Strategies for Seizing Control of Your Industry and Creating the Markets of Tomorrow,* Boston: Harvard Business School Press, 1994.

16. Ibid.
17. Ibid.
18. Ibid.
19. Patricia K. Felkins, B. J. Chakiris, and Kenneth N. Chakiris, *Change Management: A Model For Effective Organization Performance,* Quality Resources, 1993.

Bibliography

Adler, Nancy. *International Dimensions of Organizational Behavior.* Boston: Kent Publishing, 1986.

Adler, Nancy J., and Susan Bartholomew. "Managing Globally Competent People." *Academy of Management Executive*, August 1992.

Adler, Nancy J., and Fariborz Ghadar. "Human Resource Management: A Global Perspective." *Human Resource Management in International Comparison.* Rudiger Pieper, ed. Hawthorne, NY: de Gruyter, 1990.

Adler, Nancy, and Dafina N. Izraeli. *Competitive Frontiers: Women Managers in a Global Economy. International Business, 1994.*

Adler, Nancy, and Dafina N. Izraeli, eds. *Women in Management Worldwide.* Armonk, NY: M.E. Sharpe, 1988.

Adler, Nancy, and R. B. Peterson. "Expatriate Selection and Failure." *Human Resource Planning*, vol. 14, 1991.

AFS Orientation Handbook, Vol. IV. American Field Service, 1984.

Akande, Adebowale. "A Programme for Training Trainers in Nigeria." *Industrial & Commercial Training*, 1991.

Albert, Michel. *Capitalism Contre Capitalism.* Paris: Edition de Seuil, 1991.

Ali-Ali, Salahaldeen. "The Role of Training and Education in Technology Transfer: A Case Study of Kuwait." *Technovation*, 1988.

Andrews, D. H., and L. A. Goodson. "A Comparative Analysis of Models of Instructional Design." *Journal of Instructional Development*, vol. 3, 1980.

Anguo, L., and Cukier, W. *Telecommunications and Business Competitiveness.* Canada Department of Communications, 1992.

Anonymous. "Britain: Getting Into Training." *Economist*, January 25, 1992.

―――. "Language Training." *Personnel Management Plus*, May 1991.

―――. "Taking the Cultural Blinkers Off." *Business Korea*, December 1991.

―――. "Training in the 90s: The Labour Force Development Strategy (Canada)." *Worklife Report*, 1991.

————."Workforce Quality: Perspectives from the U.S. and Japan, International Symposium." U.S. Department of Labor Proceedings, 1991.

Anthony, Peg, and Lincoln A. Norton. "Link HR to Corporate Strategy." *Personnel Journal,* April 1991.

Applegate, L. M. (Frito-Lay, Inc.) *A Strategic Transition (Consolidated).* Boston: Harvard Business School Press, 1992.

Ardagh, John. *Germany and the Germans,* London: Penguin Books, 1991.

Argyris, Chris. "Teaching Smart People How to Learn." *Harvard Business Review*, May-June 1991.

Arkin, Anat. "Insuring Against Insularity." *Personnel Management*, June 1991.

Armstrong, Richard N. "Cross-Cultural Communication Training in Business: A Sensitizing Model." Eastern Michigan University Report, 1988.

Arvidson, Lars, and Kjell Rubenson. "Education and Training of the Labor Force in the EFTA Countries." Report prepared to the seminar "New Challenges in the Education and Training of the European Workforce" (Stockholm, Sweden, June 13-14, 1990), National Swedish Board Education, Stockholm, 1991.

Associated Press. "Flagging a Problem." *The Dallas Morning News,* June 8, 1994.

Atkinson, Marcia. "Build Learning into Work." *HR Magazine,* September 1994.

Atiyyah, Hamid S. "Effectiveness of Management Training in Arab Countries." *Journal of Management Development,* 1991.

Austin, Clyde, ed. *Cross-cultural Re-entry*. Abilene Christian University Press, 1986.

Baden-Fuller, Charles, and John M. Stopford. *Rejuvenating the Mature Business*. London: Routledge, 1992.

Barham, Kevin and Marion Devine. *The Quest for the International Manager: Survey of Global Human Resource Strategies.* London: Business International Press, 1991.

Barnlund, Dean C. *Communicative Styles of Japan and America: Images and Realities.* Belmont, CA: Wadsworth, 1989.

Barnum, Cynthia, and David R. Gaster. "Global Leadership." *Executive Excellence*, June 1991.

Barsoux, Jean Louis, and Peter Lawrence. *Management in France.* London: Cassell, 1990.

Bartlett, Christopher A., and Sumantra Ghoshal. *Cross-Border Management.* Burr Ridge, IL: Business One Irwin, 1992.

————. *Managing Across Borders.* Boston: Harvard Business School Press, 1991.

————. "What Is a Global Manager?" *Harvard Business Review,* September-October 1992.

Battaglia, Beverly A. "Skills for Managing Multicultural Teams." *Cultural Diversity at Work*, January 1992.

Beamish, Paul W., J. Petter Killing, Donald J. Lecraw, and Allen J. Morrison. *International Management: Text and Cases.* Burr Ridge, Il: Richard D. Irwin Inc., 1994.

Befus, C. P. "A Multilevel Treatment Approach for Culture Shock Experienced By Sojourners." *International Journal of Intercultural Relations*, vol. 12, 1988.

Ben-Yoseph, Miriam. "Designing and Delivering Cross-Cultural Instruction." Eastern Michigan University Report, 1988.

Bennis, Warren. "Leadership in the 21st Century." *Training*, May 1990.

Bereiter, C., and M. Scardamalia. "Cognitive Coping Strategies and the Problem of 'Inert' Knowledge." *In Thinking and Learning Skills: Current Research and Open Questions.* Erlbaum, 1985.

Berger, Michael. "Building Bridges Over Cultural Rivers." *International Management* (UK). vol. 42, no. 7/8, July/August 1987.

Berry, John K. "Linking Management Development to Business Strategies." *Training & Development Journal*, August 1990.

Black, J. Stewart, Hal B. Gregersen, and Mark Mendenhall. *Global Assignments—Successfully Expatriating and Repatriating International Managers.* San Francisco: Jossey-Bass, 1992.

Black, J. Stewart, and Mark Mendenhall. "Cross-Cultural Training Effectiveness: A Review and a Theoretical Framework for Future Research." *Academy of Management Review*, vol. 15, 1990.

————. "A Practical but Theory-based Framework for Selecting Cross-Cultural Training Methods." *Human Resource Management,* Winter 1989.

Black, J. Stewart, Mark Mendenhall, and Gary R. Oddou, "Towards a Comprehensive Model of International Adjustment: An Integration of Multiple Theoretical Perspectives." *Academy of Management Review,* Vol. 16, 1991.

Black, J. Stewart, and G. K. Stephens. "The Influence of the Spouse on American Expatriate Adjustment and Intent to Stay in Pacific Rim Assignments." *Journal of Management,* vol. 15, 1989.

Blocklyn, Paul L. "Developing the International Executive." *Personnel*, March 1989.

Bloom, Helen, Roland Calori, and Phillippe de Woot. *Euromanagement: A New Style for the Global Market.* London: Kogan Page Limited, 1994.

Borisoff, Deborah, and David A. Victor. *Conflict Management: A Communication Skills Approach.* Englewood Cliffs, NJ: Prentice-Hall, 1989.

Brandt, Ellen. "Global HR." *Personnel Journal*, March 1992.

Bransford, J. D., R. Sherwood, N. Vye, and J. Reiser. "Teaching Thinking and Problem Solving." *American Psychologist,* 1986.

Brislin, R. W. *Cross-Cultural Encounters.* Tarrytown, NY: Pergamon Press, 1981.

————. et al. *Intercultural Interactions: A Practical Guide.* Beverly Hills, CA: Sage Publications, 1985.

Brockway, George M. *The End of Economic Man.* New York: HarperCollins, 1991.

Brown, A. L., J. C. Campione, and J. D. Day. "Learning To Learn: On Training Students to Learn from Texts." *Educational Researcher,* 10, 1981.

Burstein, Daniel. *Euroquake.* New York: Simon and Schuster, 1991.

Business America: The Magazine of International Trade. Washington, DC: U.S. Department of Commerce. (Published biweekly.)

Byrne, John. "Management's New Gurus." *BusinessWeek*, August 31, 1992.

CSX Intermodal. "Why Most Executives Never Make It To The Top." advertisement, *International Business,* January 1995.

Callahan, Madelyn R. "Preparing the New Global Manager." *Training & Development*, March 1989.

Calvert, Gene. *Highwire Management.* San Francisco: Jossey-Bass, 1993.

Campbell, Clifton P., and Gerald D. Cheek. "Vocational Training in Switzerland." *Journal Industrial Teacher Education*, Fall 1991.

Carnevale, Anthony Patrick. *America and the New Economy: How New Competitive Standards are Radically Changing the American Workplace.* San Francisco: Jossey-Bass, 1991.

Caropreso, Frank, ed. "Managing Globally: Key Perspectives." Conference Board, Report No. 972, 1991.

Carr, Clay. "The Three R's of Training." *Training*, June 1992.

Casmir, F. L., ed. *International and Intercultural Communication.* University Press of America, 1978.

————. *International and Intercultural Communication Annual, Volume 3.* Speech Communication Association, 1976.

————. *International and Intercultural Communication Annual, Volume 2.* Speech Communication Association, 1975.

————. *International and Intercultural Communication Annual, Volume 1.* Speech Communication Association, 1974.

Casner-Lotto, Jill. "Successful Training Strategies: Twenty-six Innovative Corporate Models." *Training Process/HRD Strategic Planning,* Jossey-Bass, 1988.

Casse, Pierre. *Training for the Multicultural Manager.* Society of Intercultural Education Training Research (SIETAR), 1982.

————. *Training for the Cross-Cultural Mind.* 2nd ed. Society of Intercultural Education Training Research (SIETAR), 1981.

Catalanello, Ralph, and John Redding. "Three Strategic Training Roles." *Training & Development Journal,* December 1989.

Caudron, Shari. "Training Ensures Success Overseas." *Personnel Journal,* December 1991.

————. "Training Helps United Go Global." *Personnel Journal,* February 1992.

Choate, Pat. *Agents of Influence.* New York: Simon and Schuster, 1990.

Chowanec, Gregory D., and Charles N. Newstrom. "The Strategic Management of International Human Resources." *Business Quarterly* (University of Western Ontario), Autumn 1991.

Clarke, Clifford C., and Douglas Lipp. *The Crisis in U.S.-based Japanese Companies: Cross-Cultural Conflict.* Yarmouth, ME: Intercultural Press, 1996.

Cocheu, Ted. "Integrating Training with Quality Strategy." *Technical & Skills Training,* February/March 1992.

Cohen, R. "Europeans Fear Unemployment Will Only Rise." *New York Times,* June 13, 1993, Sec. 1.

Cohn, Margaret. "What It Takes To Be A Global Manager in the 1990s." *Innovations in International Compensation,* August 1990.

Collins, James C., and Jerry I. Porras. *Built To Last.* New York: HarperBusiness, 1994.

Condon, J.C. *Good Neighbors, Communicating with Mexicans.* Yarmouth, ME: Intercultural Press, Inc., 1985.

Conference Board Survey 1993. Reported in Louis Uchitelle, "Strong Companies Joining Trend to Eliminate Jobs," *New York Times,* July 26, 1993.

Conference Board. *Building Global Teamwork for Growth and Survival.* The Conference Board, Research Bulletin No. 228, 1990.

Conner, Daryl R. *Managing at the Speed of Change.* New York: Villard Books, 1992.

Cooney, Barry D. "Japan and America: Culture Counts." *Training & Development Journal.* vol. 43, no. 8, August 1989.

Cooper, John. "Tailoring Education and Training to Labour Market Requirements." *International Journal of Manpower,* 1991.

Copeland, Lennie, and Lewis Briggs. *Going International: How to Make Friends and Deal Effectively in the International Marketplace.* New York: Random House, 1985.

Coupland, Lester. "Developing European Trainers." *Industrial & Commercial Training,* 1991.

Craig, Gordon A. *The Germans.* London: Penguin, 1991.

Craig, R. L., ed. *Training & Development Handbook, A Guide to Human Resource Development.* 3d ed. ASTD and McGraw-Hill, 1987.

Crump, Larry. "Japanese Managers-Western Workers: Cross-Cultural Training and Development Issues." *Journal of Management Development (UK).* vol. 8, no. 4, 1989.

Daniels, John L., and Dr. N. Caroline Daniels. *Global Vision: Building New Models for the Corporation of the Future.* New York: McGraw-Hill Inc., 1993.

Davis, S. M., and W. H. Davidson. *2020 Vision.* New York: Simon & Schuster, 1991.

deForest, Mariah E. "When in Mexico . . ." *Business Mexico,* July 1991.

Deal, Terence E., and Allen A. Kennedy. *Corporate Cultures: The Rites and Rituals of Corporate Life.* Reading, MA: Addison-Wesley, 1982.

Denton, D. Keith."Process Mapping Trims Cycle Time." *HR Magazine,* February 1995.

Desatnick, Robert L., and Margo L. Bennett. *Human Resource Management in the Multinational Company.* New York: Gower Press, 1977.

Dimancescu, D. *The Seamless Enterprise: Making Cross-Functional Management Work.* New York: Harper Business, 1992.

Doktor, Robert, ed. *International HRD Annual, Volume 1.* ASTD, 1985.

Dole, G. E. et al., eds. *Essays in the Science of Culture in Honor of Leslie A. White.* Thomas Y. Crowell Company, 1960.

Domsch, M., and B. Lichtenberger. "Managing the Global Manager: Predeparture Training and Development for German Expatriates in China and Brazil." *Journal of Management Development,* 1991.

Doz, Yves. *Strategic Management in International Companies.* Tarrytown, NY: Pergamon Press, 1986.

Doz, Y. L., C. A. Bartlett, and C. K. Prahalad. "Global Competitive Pressures vs. Host Country Demands: Managing the Tensions in Multinational Corporations." *California Management Review,* 23, no. 3, 1981.

———. "Controlled Variety: A Challenge for Human Resource Management in the Multinational Corporation." *Human Resource Management,* 25, no. 1, 1986.

Doz, Y. L., and C. K. Prahalad. *Multinational Companies' Missions: Balancing National Responsiveness and Global Integration.* New York: The Free Press, 1987.

Drucker, Peter. "The New Society of Organizations." *Harvard Business Review,* September-October 1992.

Dunbar, E., and M. Ehrlich. *International Human Resource Practices, Selecting, Training, and Managing the International Staff: A Survey Report.* The Project on International Human Resources. Columbia University-Teachers College, 1986.

Early, P. C. "Intercultural Training for Managers: A Comparison of Documentary and Interpersonal Methods." *Academy of Management Journal,* 30.

"East Asian Miracle." Editorial. *Far Eastern Economic Review,* October 21, 1993.

Elashmawi, Farid. "Multicultural Management: A Key for the Success of Indonesian Petroleum Joint Ventures." Proceedings Indonesian Petroleum Association, 23rd Annual Convention, October 1994.

Europe: The Magazine of the European Community. Washington, DC: EC Delegation to the United States. (10 times per year)

Europe: World Partner—The External Relations of the European Community. Luxembourg: Office for Official Publications of the European Communities, 1991.

The European Community 1992 and Beyond. Luxembourg: Office for Official Publications of the European Communities, 1991.

The European Community in the Nineties. Washington, DC: EC Delegation to the United States, 1992.

Evans, P. A. L. "Strategies for Human Resource Management in Complex Multinational Corporations: A European Perspective." In V. Pucik's Academy of Management Proposal, *Emerging Human Resource Management Strategies in Multinational Firms: A Tricontinental Perspective,* 1987.

————. "The Strategic Outcomes of Human Resource Management." *Human Resource Management,* 25, 1, 1986.

Evans, Paul, Yves Doz, and Andre Laurent, eds. *Human Resource Management in International Firms: Change, Globalization, Innovation.* New York: St. Martin's Press, 1990.

Felkins, Patricia Kay, B. J. Chakiris, and Kenneth N. Chakiris. "Global Consultation." *In Change Consultation.* Quality Resources Press, 1993.

Felkins, Patricia K., B. J. Chakiris, and Kenneth N. Chakiris. *Change Management: A Model For Effective Organization Performance.* Quality Resources, 1993.

Ferguson, Henry. *Tomorrow's Global Executive.* Burr Ridge, IL: Dow Jones-Irwin, 1988.

Filipczak, Bob. "The Business of Training at NCR." *Training,* February 1992.

Fisher, Anne B. "How to Make a Merger Work." *Fortune,* January 24, 1994.

Fisher, G. *International Negotiation, A Cross-Cultural Perspective.* Yarmouth, ME: Intercultural Press, Inc., 1980.

Fisher, Glen. Mindsets: *The Role of Culture and Perception in International Relations.* Yarmouth, ME: Intercultural Press, 1988.

Fitz-enz, Jac. *Human Value Management.* San Francisco: Jossey-Bass, 1990.

Fitzgerald, Patricia L. "HRD for the Global Age." *Training & Development Journal,* June 1987.

Flores, J. "The Fiber Optic Transmission Equipment Market in Mexico."
    U.S. Commerce Department, American Embassy, Mexico City,
    September 1992. Cited in *Mexico Business Monthly*, February 1993a.
————. "The Telecommunications Equipment Market in Mexico." U.S.
    Commerce Department, American Embassy, Mexico City, January
    1993. Cited in *Mexico Business Monthly*, February 1993b.
Flynn, Brian H. "The Challenge of Multinational Sales Training." *Training
    & Development Journal.* vol. 41, no. 11, November 1987.
Foeman, Anita K. "Managing Multiracial Institutions: Goals and
    Approaches for Race-Relations Training." *Communication Education*,
    July 1991.
————. "Race-Relations Training as the Asking of Questions." Paper
    presented at the 1991 annual meeting of the Eastern Communication
    Association, April 1991.
Fombrun, Charles, Noel M. Tichy, and Marry Anne Devana. *Strategic
    Human Resource Management.* New York: John Wiley & Sons, 1984.
Frank, Eric, and Roger Bennett. "HRD in Eastern Europe." *Journal of
    European Industrial Training*, 1991.
Frankenstein, John, and Hassan Hosseini. "Essential Training for Japanese
    Duty." *Management Review.* vol. 77, no. 7, July 1988.
Frederick, Howard. *Global Communication and Internaitonal Relations.*
    Belmont, CA: Wadsworth Publishing Company, 1993.
Furnham, A., and S. Bochner. *Culture Shock: Psychological Reactions to
    Unfamiliar.* London: Methuen, 1986.
Gagne, R. M., and R. Glaser. "Foundations in Learning Research," in
    Instructional Techniques: Foundations. Erlbaum, 1987.
Galagan, Patricia A. "Executive Development in a Changing World."
    Training & Development, June 1990.
Galagan, Patricia. "The Learning Organization Made Plain." *Training
    and Development Journal*, 45, no. 10, October 1991.
Galbraith, J. R., and E. E. Lawler and Associates. *Organizing for the Future:
    The New Logic for Managing Complex Organizations.* San Francisco:
    Jossey-Bass, 1993.
Galinski, E., J. T. Bond, and D. E. Friedman. *The Changing Workforce.*
    New York: Families and Work Institute, 1993.
Gardenswartz, Lee, and Anita Rowe. "Elements of Culture Impact
    Teamwork." International HR/Supplement, *HR News,* January 1995.
Gayeski, Diane M., Ed Nathan, and Jon Sickle. "Creating a CBT System
    for Multinational Training." *Interactive Learning International*,
    January-March 1992.
Geber, Beverly. "The Care and Breeding of Global Managers." *Training*,
    July 1992.
————. "A Global Approach to Training." *Training*, vol. 26, no. 9,
    September 1989.

Ghadar, Fariborz, Philip D. Grub, Robert T. Moran, and Marshall Geer. *Global Business Management in the 1990s.* Washington, DC: Beacham Publishing, Inc., 1990.

Gilbert, Nathaniel. "Insulation From Culture Shock: Prepping Employees for Living Overseas." *Trainer's Workshop.* vol. 2, no. 4, October 1987.

Gilley, Jerry W. *Strategic Planning for Human Resource Development.* ASTD *Info-Line*, June 1992.

Gitter, Robert J. "Job Training in Europe: Lessons From Abroad." *Monthly Labor Review*, April 1992.

Glover, W. G., and G. W. Shames. *World-Class Service.* Yarmouth, ME: Intercultural Press, 1989.

Goldstein, Alan. "A Team Player." *The Dallas Morning News,* March 28, 1995.

Goodman,Michael B. *Working in a Global Environment: Understanding, Communicating, and Managing Transnationally.* Piscataway, NJ: IEEE, 1995.

Goold, M., *Strategic Control.* The Economist Books/Business Books, London, 1990.

Gordon, Colin. "The Business Culture of France." *Business Cultures of Europe*, Collin Randlesome, ed. Oxford: Heinemann, 1990.

Gray, P., L. Olfman, and H. Park. "The Interface Problem in International Group DDS." paper presented for the task force on International Group Decision Support Systems at the 21st Hawaii International Conference in Systems Sciences, Honolulu, January 5-7, 1988.

Gregersen, Hal B. "Commitments to a Parent Company and a Local Work Unit During Repatriation." *Personnel Psychology*, Spring 1992.

Gregersen, Hal, and J. Stewart Black. "When Yankee Comes Home: Factors Related to Expatriate and Spouse Repatriation Adjustment." *Journal of International Business Studies*, vol. 22, 1991.

Greising, David. "Globe Trotter: If it's 5:30, this must be Tel Aviv." *Business Week,* October 17, 1994.

Griffin, Trenholme J., and W. Russell Daggatt. "The Global Negotiator: Building Strong Business Relationships Anywhere in the World." *Harper Business*, 1990.

Gross, Thomas, Ernie Turner, and Lars Cederholm. "Building Teams for Global Operations." *Management Review,* June 1987.

Grove, Cornelius, and Constance Franklin. "Using the Right Fork Is Just the Beginning: Intercultural Training in the Global Era." *International Public Relations Review 13*, no. 1, 1990.

Gudykunst, W. B., M. R. Hammer, and R. L. Wiseman. "An Analysis of an Integrated Approach to Cross-Cultural Training." *International Journal of Intercultural Relations, no 1, 1977.*

Hales, Larry D. "Training: A Product of Business Planning." *Training & Development Journal*, July 1986.

Hall, Edward T. *Beyond Culture.* New York: Doubleday Anchor Books, 1976, and Geert Hofstede, *Culture's Consequences: International Differences in Work-Related Values.*

Hall, E. T., and Hall, M. R. *Understanding Cultural Differences: Germans, French, and Americans.* Yarmouth, ME: Intercultural Press, 1990.

Hall, Edward T. *Beyond Culture.* New York: Anchor Press/Doubleday, 1976.

Hall, Edward T. *The Cultures of France and Germany.* New York: Intercultural Press, 1989.

―――. *Dance of Life: The Other Dimensions of Time.* New York: Anchor, Doubleday, 1983.

―――. *Hidden Differences: Doing Business with the Japanese.* New York: Doubleday, 1987.

―――. *The Silent Language.* New York: Doubleday, 1989.

Hamel, Gary and C. K. Prahalad. *Competing for the Future: Breakthrough Strategies for Seizing Control of Your Industry and Creating the Markets of Tomorrow.* Boston: *Harvard Business School Press,* 1994.

―――. "Strategic Intent." *Harvard Business Review*, May-June 1989.

Hammonds, Keith H., Kevin Kelly, and Karen Thurston. "The New World of Work." *Business Week,* October 17, 1994.

Hampden-Turner, Charles M. *Charting the Corporate Mind: From Dilemma to Strategy.* Oxford: Basil Blackwell, 1990.

Hampden-Turner, C. *Creating Culture: From Discord to Harmony.* International Management Series. Reading, MA: Addison-Wesley, 1990b.

Hampden-Turner, Charles, and Alfons Trompenaars. *The Seven Cultures of Capitalism: Value Systems for Creating Wealth in the United States, Japan, Germany, France, Britain, Sweden, and The Netherlands.* New York: Doubleday, 1993.

Hampden-Turner, C., P. Evans, et al (eds.), *Human Resource Management in Intercultural Firms.* New York: St. Martin's Press, 1990a.

Handy, Charles. *The Age of Unreason.* London: Century Hutchison, 1989.

Harbrecht, Douglas, Geri Smith, and Gail DeGeorge. "Ripping Down Walls Across the Americas." *Business Week.* December 26, 1994.

Harris, Philip R. and Robert T. Moran. *Managing Cultural Differences,* 2nd ed., Houston: Gulf Publishing, 1989.

Harris, Philip R., and Robert T. Moran. *Managing Cultural Differences: High-Performance Strategies for a New World of Business.* Houston: Gulf Publishing Company, 1993.

Harris, P. R., and R. T. Moran. *Managing Cultural Differences.* 2nd ed. Gulf Publishing Co., 1987.

Hart, P. E., and A. Shipman. "Financing Training in Britain." *National Institute Economic Review*, May 1991.

Hawk, Elizabeth J. "Culture and Rewards." *Personnel Journal,* April 1995.

Hays, R. D. "Expatriate Selection: Ensuring Success and Avoiding Failure." *Journal of International Business Studies*, Spring 1974.

Hedlund, Gunnar, and D. Rolander. "Action in Heterarchies: New Approaches in Managing the MNC," in *Managing the Global Firm*, G. Hedlund, C. Bartlett, and Y. Doz. eds. London: Routledge, 1990.

Hemphill, David F. "Thinking Hard About Culture in Adult Education: Not a Trivial Pursuit." *Adult Learning*, May 1992.

Hill, Richard. *EuroManagers & Martians: The Business Cultures of Europe's Trading Nations*. Brussels: Europublications, 1994.

————. *We Europeans*. Brussels: Europublications, 1992.

Hirschhorn, L. *Managing in the New Team Environment*. Reading, MA: Addison-Wesley, 1991.

Hirschhorn, L., and T. Gilmore. "The New Boundaries of the Boundaryless Company." *Harvard Business Review,* May-June 1992.

Hodgson, Kent. "Adapting Ethical Decisions to a Global Marketplace," *Management Review,* May 1992

Hofstede, Geert. *Culture's Consequences: International Differences in Work Related Values*. Beverly Hills, CA: Sage, 1980.

————. *Cultures and Organizations: Software of the Mind*. Beverly Hills, CA: McGraw-Hill, 1991.

Hofstein, William J. *The Japanese Power Game: What It Means for Americans*. New York: Charles Scribner and Sons, 1990.

Hoopes, David S., and Paul Ventura, eds. *Intercultural Sourcebook: Cross-Cultural Training Methodologies*. Yarmouth, ME: Intercultural Press, 1979.

Humphrey, Vernon. "Training the Total Organization." *Training & Development Journal*, October 1990.

Ioannou, Lori. "Stateless Executives." *International Business,* February 1995.

Ibe, Masanobu, and Noriko Sato. "Educating Japanese Leaders for a Global Age: The Role of the International Education Center." *Journal of Management Development (UK)*. vol. 8, no. 4, 1989.

Iyer, S. C. "Problems of Management Development in the Indian Subcontinent." *Journal of Management Development,* 1991.

Jacobs, Michael T. *Short-term America*. Boston: Harvard Business School Press, 1991.

Jacques, Elliot, and Stephen D. Clement, *Executive Leadership: A Practical Guide to Managing Complexity*. Basil Blackwell, 1991.

Jenkins, Alan. "Training and HR Strategy in France: Discourse and Reality." *Employee Relations*, 1991.

Johansen, R., et al. *Leading Business Teams: How Teams Can Use Technology and Group Process Tools to Enhance Performance*. Addison-Wesley Series on Organizational Development. Reading, MA.: Addison-Wesley, 1991.

Johnson & Johnson. "Social Responsibility In Action Worldwide."

Johnson, Keith R. "Organizational Development in a Context of Opposed Cultural Values: The Case of O.D. in Venezuela." *Organization Development Journal*, Winter 1990.

Johnson, Philip. "Transcending Cultural Differences Through Experiential Teaching Techniques." *Adult Learning*, November 1991.

Johnston, Anton, and Hallgerd Dyrssen. "Cooperation in the Development of Public Sector Management Skills: The SIDA Experience." *Journal of Management Development*, 1991.

Johnston, William B. "Global Workforce 2000: The New World Labor Market." *Harvard Business Review*, March-April 1991.

Jones, Merrick L. "Management Development: An African Focus." *International Studies of Management and Organization.* vol. 19, no. 1, Spring 1989.

Juechter, W. Mathew. "What it Really Takes to Transform a Company." ARC International, Ltd., 1993.

Katzenbach, J. R., and D. K. Smith. *The Wisdom of Teams.* Boston: Harvard Business School Press, 1993.

Kennedy, Gavin. *Negotiate Anywhere!: How to Succeed in International Markets.* New York: Arrow Books, 1987.

Keys, Bernard, and Robert Wells. "A Global Management Development Laboratory for a Global World." *Journal of Management Development*, 1992.

Kiechel, W. "How We Will Work in the Year 2000." *Fortune,* May 17, 1993.

Kidder, Rushworth. *How Good People Make Tough Choices.* New York: William Morrow, 1995.

Kinlaw, Dennis C. *Developing Superior Work Teams.* University Associates, 1991.

Kobrin, S. J. "Expatriate Reduction and Strategic Control in American Multinational Corporations." *Human Resource Management*, 27, no. 1, 1986.

Kohls, L. R. *Survival Kit for Overseas Living.* 2nd ed. Yarmouth, ME: Intercultural Press, 1984.

Koopman, Albert. *Transcultural Management: How to Unlock Global Resources.* Cambridge, MA: Basil Blackwell, 1991.

Korn/Ferry International and Columbia School of Business. *21st Century Report: Reinventing the CEO.* Korn/Ferry International, 1989.

Kotkin, J. *Tribue: How Race, Religion, and Identity Determine Success in the New Global Economy.* New York: Random House, 1993.

Kras, Eva S. *Management in Two Cultures: Bridging the Gap between U.S. and Mexican Managers.* Yarmouth, ME: Intercultural Press, 1989.

Kupfer, Andrew. "How to be a Global Manager." *Fortune,* March 14, 1988.

Laabs, Jennifer. "Whirlpool Managers Become Global Architects." *Personnel Journal*, December 1991.

Lamont, Douglas. *Winning Worldwide: Strategies for Dominating Global Markets*. Burr Ridge, IL: Business One Irwin, 1991.

Landis, D., and R. Brislin. *Handbook on Intercultural Training*, Volume 1. Tarrytown, NY: Pergamon Press, 1983.

Lanier, A. R. "Selection and Preparation for Overseas Transfers." *Personnel Journal*, 58, 1979.

Landau, Nilly. "Face to Face Marketing is Best." *International Business,* June 1994.

Latham, G. "Human Resource Training and Development." *Annual Review of Psychology,* 39, 1988.

Laurent, André. "The Cross-Cultural Puzzle of International Human Resource Management." *Human Resource Management,* vol. 25, no. 1, 1986.

————. "Cross-Cultural Management for Pan-European Companies." *Europe 1992 and Beyond.* Spyros Makridakis, ed. San Francisco: Jossey Bass, 1991.

Lazer, Robert I. "Steering Through Turbulence." *Training & Development*, December 1991.

Lee Smith, "Stamina: Who Has it, Why You Need it, How You Get it." *Fortune,* November 28, 1994.

Leuenberger, Niklaus. "The Fundamentals Never Change." *Profit Magazine,* September/October 1994.

Liu, H., et al. *Quantum Leap.* San Francisco: United States-China Educational Institute, Spring 1992.

Lobel, Sharon A. "Global Leadership Competencies: Managing to a Different Drumbeat." *Human Resource Management* 29, no. 1, Spring 1990.

Lorange, P. "Human Resource Management in Multinational Cooperative Ventures." *Human Resource Management,* 25, no. 1, 1986.

Lorenz, Christopher. "The Birth of the 'Transnational." *The McKinsey Quarterly*, Autumn 1989.

Lubove, Seth. "Ovo Je Line Extension." *Forbes*, July 22, 1991.

Maccoby, Michael, ed. *Sweden at the Edge*. Philadelphia: University of Pennsylvania Press, 1991.

Makridakis, Spyros, ed. *Europe 1992 and Beyond*. San Francisco: Jossey-Bass, 1990.

Makridakis, Spyros G. et al. *Single Market Europe: Opportunities and Challenges for Business*. San Francisco: Jossey-Bass, 1991.

Maljers, Floria A. "Inside Unilever: The Evolving Transnational Company." *The Harvard Business Review*, September–October, 1992.

Manzini, A. O., and J. D. Gridley. *Integrating Human Resources and Strategic Business Planning*. New York: AMACOM, 1986.

Markovitz, David C. "Total Quality Training." *Technical & Skills Training.* ASTD, April 1992.

Marquardt, Michael J., ed. *International HRD,* Volume 3. Alexandria, VA: ASTD, 1987.

Marquardt, Michael and Angus Reynolds. *The Global Learning Organization.* Burr Ridge, IL: Irwin, 1994.

Marquardt, Michael, and Dean Engel. *Global Human Resource Development.* Englewood Cliffs, NJ: Prentice-Hall, 1993.

Marsick, Victoria J., and Lars Cederholm. "Developing Leadership in International Managers—An Urgent Challenge!" *The Columbia Journal of World Business XXII,* no. 4, Winter 1988.

Martin, B. "Internalizing Instructional Design." *Educational Technology,* 24, 1984.

Mathews, Jay. "In search of profits...shares in Tom Peter's 'Excellence' companies fail to match S&P 500." *The Dallas Morning News,* November 21, 1994.

McLearn, Gary N., and Barbara S. Arney. "Advanced Trainers Development Workshop (Islamabad, Pakistan, July 7-26, 1990). Final Report." *Academy for Educational Development,* August 1990.

Mendenhall, Mark, E. Dunbar, and G. Oddou. "Expatriate Selection, Training, and Career-pathing: A Review and Critique." *Human Resource Management,* 26, 1978.

Mendenhall, Mark E., and Gary R. Oddou. "Acculturation Profiles of Expatriate Managers: Implications for Cross-cultural Training Programs." *Columbia Journal of World Business, Volume 21,* 1986.

———. "The Dimensions of Expatriate Acculturation: A Review. *Academy of Management Review,* 10, no. 1, 1985.

Mervosh, Edward M. Editorial, *International Business,* July 1994.

Mervosh, Edward M. "Boss's Bold New Boss." *International Business,* December 1994.

Middleton, John. "Vocational and Technical Education and Training. A World Bank Policy Paper." ERIC Document No. ED334454. A report by the International Bank for Reconstruction and Development, 1991.

———. "World Bank Support for Vocational Education and Training: New Directions for the 1990s." *Journal Industrial Teacher Education,* Spring 1991.

Miles, Gregory L. "Managing Explosive Foreign Growth." *International Business,* June 1994.McEnery, Jean and Gaston DesHarnais. "Culture Shock." *Training & Development Journal,* April 1990.

Miles, Gregory L. "Marriages of Convenience," *International Business,* January 1995.

———. "Multinational Future Shock." *International Business,* December 1994.

————. "The Trials of Two Acquirers." *International Business,* February, 1995.

Miller, E. L., S. Beechler, B. Bhatt, and R. Nath. "The Relationship Between the Global Strategic Planning Process and the Human Resource Management Function." *Human Resource Planning,* 9, no.1, 1986.

Miller, Vincent A. *The Guidebook for International Trainers in Business and Industry.* New York: Van Nostrand Reinhold and ASTD, 1979.

Milliman, John, Mary A. Von Glinow, and Maria Nathan. "Organizational Life Cycles and Strategic International Human Resource Management in Multinational Companies: Implications for Congruence Theory." April 1991.

Misa, K. R., and J. M. Fabricatore. "Return on Investment of Overseas Personnel." *Financial Executive,* April, 1979.

Mitchell, Mary. ""Managing Multicultural Project Teams Within The European Union." American Graduate School of International Management (Thunderbird) research paper, December 7, 1994.

Mitroff, Ian I. *Business Not as Usual.* San Francisco: Jossey-Bass Publishers, 1987.

Montville, Joseph V. *Conflict and Peacemaking in Multiethnic Societies.* New York: Lexington Books, 1990.

Moran, Robert, and William Stripp. *International Negotiation.* Houston: Gulf Publishing, 1991.

Moran, Robert T., "Airbus: An Exceptional Multi-Cultural Success." *International Management,* February 1989.

————. "Making Globalization Work." *World Executive's Digest,* January 1993.

Morgan, Gareth. *Riding the Waves of Change: Developing Managerial Competencies for a Turbulent World.* San Francisco: Jossey-Bass, 1988.

Morgan, Patrick. "International HRM: Fact or Fiction?" *Personnel Administrator,* September 1986.

Morical, Keith, and Benhong Tsai. "Adapting Training for Other Cultures." *Training & Development,* April 1992.

Morris, Desmond. *Gestures.* Gainesville, FL: Triad/Granada Press, 1981.

Morton, Michael. *The Corporation of the 1990s.* New York: Oxford University Press, 1991.

Moulton, Harper. "Executive Development and Education: An Evaluation." *Journal of Management Development,* 9, no. 4, 1991.

Murray, F. T., and A. H. Murray. "Global Managers for Global Businesses." *Sloan Management Review,* 27, no. 2, 1986.

Murray, Margo, ed., et al. "The 1992 Global Connector: The Complete Resource Directory for International Training & Development." *Annual Directory of International Training Associations, Institutions, Societies, and Training and Consulting Firms,* 1992.

Nadler, L., ed. *The Handbook of Human Resource Development*. New York: John Wiley & Sons, 1984.

Nadler, Leonard and Zeace Nadler. "Overcoming the Language Barrier." *Training & Development Journal*, June 1987.

Naik, G. "Beyond the Borders." *Wall Street Journal*, Executive Education Supplement, September 10, 1993.

Naisbitt, John, and Patricia Aburdene. *Megatrends 2000: Ten New Directions for the 1990s*. New York: William Morrow and Co. Inc., 1990.

Neale, Rosemary, and Richard Mindel. "Rigging Up Multicultural Teamworking." *Personnel Management*, January 1992.

Nelson, G. L. "The Implications of Schema Theory Reading Research to Technology Transfer in Developing Countries." In *Proceedings of the Human Factors Society – 34th Annual Meeting,* 1990.

Noel, James L., and Ram Charan, "GE Brings Global Thinking to Light." *Training & Development*, June 1992.

O'Connor, Robert. "Britain Trains to Compete in a Unified Europe." *Personnel Journal*, May 1991.

O'Connor, Robert. "New Training Approaches for Europe '93." *Personnel Journal*, May 1992.

O'Hara-Devereaux, Mary, and Robert Johansen. *GlobalWork: Bridging Distance, Culture & Time*. San Francisco: Jossey-Bass, 1994.

O'Keefe, Bill. "Adopting Multimedia on a Global Scale." *Instruction Delivery Systems*, September/October 1991.

Oddou, Gary R. "Managing Your Expatriates: What the Successful Firms Do." *Human Resource Planning,* 1991.

Odenwald, Sylvia. *Global Training: How to Design a Training Program for the Multinational Corporation*. Burr Ridge, IL: Business One Irwin, 1993.

Ogden, John D. "Designing Cross-Cultural Orientation Programs for Business." Eastern Michigan University Report, 1988.

Ohmae, Kenichi. *The Borderless World*. New York: Harper Business Press, 1990.

Owen, Harrison. *Riding the Tiger: Doing Business in a Transforming World*. Potomac, MD: Abbott Publishing, 1991.

Palmlund, Thord. "UNDP's Management Development Programme." *Journal of Management Development,* 1991.

Parry, Scott B. "Linking Training to the Business Plan." *Training & Development,* May, 1991.

Pascale, Richard. *Managing on the Edge*. New York: Simon and Schuster, 1990.

Peak, Martha H. "Developing an International Management Style." *Management Review*, February 1991.

Pedersen, Paul. *A Handbook for Developing Multicultural Awareness.* American Association for Counseling and Development, 1988.

Pfizer Inc. and The Pfizer Foundation, Inc."1992 Contributions Report."

Phatak, A. V. *International Dimensions of Management.* 2nd ed. Boston: PWS-Kent Publishing Co., 1989.

Phillips, Nicola. *From Vision To Beyond Teamwork: 10 Ways to Wake Up And Shake Up Your Company.* Burr Ridge, IL: Irwin Professional Publishing, 1995.

————. *Managing International Teams.* Burr Ridge, IL: Richard D. Irwin, Inc., 1994.

Plihal, Jane, and Jeanette Daines. "How to Succeed in an Overseas Assignment." *Vocational Education Journal.* vol. 63, no. 3, April 1988.

Porter, Michael E. *The Competitive Advantage of Nations.* New York: Free Press, 1990.

Prahalad, C. K., and Yves Doz. *The Multinational Mission: Balancing Local Demands and Global Vision.* New York: Free Press, 1987.

Pucik, Vladimir. "Strategic Alliances, Organizational Learning, and Competitive Advantage: The HRM Agenda." *Human Resource Management*, Spring 1988.

Ralston, D. A., D. J. Gustafson, P. M. Elsass, and R. H. Terpstra. "Eastern Values: A Comparison of Managers in the United States, Hong Kong, and the People's Republic of China. *Journal of Applied Psychology,* 77, no. 5, 1992.

Randolph, Benton. "When Going Global Isn't Enough." Randlesome, Collin, ed. *Business Cultures of Europe.* London: Heinemann, 1990.

Rapaport, Richard. "To Build a Winning Team: An Interview with Head Coach Bill Walsh." *Harvard Business Review.* January-February 1993.

Ray, Michael. "The Emerging New Paradigm in Business." In *New Traditions in Business Spirit & Leadership in the 21st Century.* ed. John Renesch. San Francisco: New Leaders Publications, 1991.

Reich, Robert B. "Who is Them?" *Harvard Business Review*, March-April 1991.

————. "Who is Us?" *Harvard Business Review*, January-February 1990.

————. *The Work of Nations: Preparing Ourselves for 21st Century Capitalism.* Alfred A. Knopf, 1991.

Reynolds, Angus, and Leonard Nadler. *The Global HRD Consultant's and Practitioner's Handbook.* Amherst, MA: HRD Press, 1993.

Rhinesmith, Stephen H. *A Manager's Guide to Globalization.* Burr Ridge, IL: Business One Irwin, 1992.

————. "An Agenda for Globalization." *Training & Development,* February 1991.

————. "Developing Intercultural Sensitivity." *Training & Culture Newsletter*, February/March, 1992.

————. "Going Global from the Inside Out." *Training and Development,* November 1991.

Rhinesmith, Stephen H., John N. Williamson, David M. Ehlen, and Denise S. Maxwell. "Developing Leaders for a Global Enterprise." *Training and Development Journal*, April 1989.

Rhodeback, Melanie, Wen Ben-Lai, and Louis P. White. "Ethical Consideration in Organization Development: An Empirical Approach." *Organization Development Journal*, Winter 1990.

Richter, Alan, and Cynthia Barnum. "When Values Clash." *HR Magazine,* September 1994.

Ricks, David A. *Big Business Blunders: Mistakes in Multinational Marketing.* Burr Ridge, IL: Dow Jones-Irwin, 1983.

Rigby, J. Malcolm. "The Challenge of Multinational Team Development." *Journal of Management Development.* vol. 6, no. 3, 1987.

Rimalower, George P. "Translation, Please." *Training & Development*, February 1992.

Rothwell, Sheila. "The Development of the International Manager." *Personnel Management*, January 1992.

San, Gee. "Enterprise Training in Taiwan: Results from the Vocational Training Needs Survey." *Economics of Education Review*, 1990.

Saporito, Bill. "The Eclipse of Mars." *Fortune,* November 28, 1994.

Savona, Dave "Can Foreigners Save L.A. Gear?" *International Business,* December 1994.

————. "Changing the Rules." *International Business.* January 1993.

Savich, Richard S., and Waymond Rodgers. "Assignments Overseas: Easing the Transition Before and After." *Personnel.* vol. 65, no. 8, August 1988.

Schleger, Peter R. "Making International Videos: An Odyssey." *Training & Development*, February 1992.

Schloss, Sylvia. "Training: From Lay-Bys to Languages." *Industrial Society*, June 1991.

Scullion, Hugh. "Why Companies Prefer to Use Expatriates." *Personnel Management,* November 1991.

Senge, Peter. *The Fifth Discipline.* New York: Doubleday, 1990.

Setliff, Rebecca J., and Lori A. Taft. "Intensive Language and Culture Orientation Program for Japan." Eastern Michigan University Proceedings, 1988.

Shaeffer, Ruth G. "Building Global Teamwork for Growth and Survival." *The Conference Board Research Bulletin,* no. 228.

Sherman, Stratford. "Andy Grove: How Intel Makes Spending Pay Off." *Fortune,* February 22, 1993.

Sheth, Jagdish, and Golpira Eshghi, eds. *Global Human Resource Perspectives*. South-Western Publishing, 1989.

"SIETAR: Exploring Cultural Content." *HR Reporter*, vol. 6, no. 10, October 1989.

Silberman, M. *Active Training*. New York: Lexington Books, 1990.

Silha, Stephen. "The Future Isn't What It Used To Be." *Creative Living,* Winter 1993.

Simnacher, Betsy. "Donations help schools keep up with computers," *The Dallas Morning News,* January 17, 1995.

Silverman, Suzann D. "Reporting in Tongues." *International Business,* November 1994.

Silvestre, Jean J. "Schooling and Vocational Training in Switzerland." *OECD Observer,* June/July 1991.

Singer, Marshall R. *Intercultural Communication: A Perceptual Approach.* New York: Prentice Hall (Simon & Shuster), 1987.

Smith, C. E. *Disappearing Border: Mexico-United States Relations to the 1990s.* Stanford, CA.: Stanford University Press, 1992.

Smith, Lee. "Stamina: Who Has it, Why You Need it, How You Get it." *Fortune,* November 28, 1994.

Snelbecker, G. E. "Global Concepts: An Instructional Perspective-Differentiated Instructional Systems Design (DISD)." Presented at the 47th Annual Conference of the American Society for Training and Development.

Stacey, Ralph D. *Managing Chaos: Dynamic Business Strategies in an Unpredictable World.* London: Kogan Page, Ltd., 1992.

Starkey, Judith A. "Diversity: An Accelerating Workforce Reality." *The Illinois Manufacturer*, May/June 1994.

Steinberg, Carl. "Train in Vain?" *World Trade*, March 1992.

Stewart, Edward C., and Milton J. Bennett. *American Cultural Patterns: A Cross-Cultural Perspective.* rev.ed. Yarmouth, ME: Intercultural Press, 1991.

Stewart, Thomas A. "How To Lead A Revolution." *Fortune,* November 28, 1994.

Stewart, Thomas A. "How to Manage in the Global Era." *Fortune*, January 15, 1990.

Stone, R. J. "Expatriate Selection and Failure." *Human Resource Planning*, 14, no. 1, 1991.

Storey, John. "Do the Japanese Make Better Managers?" *Personnel Management*, August 1991.

Storti, C. *The Art of Crossing Cultures.* Yarmouth, ME: Intercultural Press, 1990.

Stringer, Donna, and Linda Taylor. "Guidelines for Implementing Diversity Training." *Training & Culture Newsletter*, May 1991.

Stuart, Karen D. "Teens Play a Role in Moves Overseas." *Personnel Journal*, March 1992.

Stuart, Peggy. "Global Outlook Brings Good Things to GE Medical." *Personnel Journal*, June 1992.

Suzuki, Norihiko. "The Attributes of Japanese CEOs: Can They be Trained?" *Journal of Management Development (UK)*. vol. 8, no. 4, 1989.

Swaak, Reyer (Rick) A. "Global Competition Changes Old Habits And Thinking." International HR/Supplement to *HR News*, January 1995.

Swierczek, Fredric W. "Culture and Training: How Do They Play Away From Home?" *Training & Development Journal*. vol. 42, no. 11, November 1988.

Tachiki, Dennis S. "Japanese Management Going Transnational." *Journal for Quality and Participation*, December 1991.

Taylor, Craig, and Fredric Frank. "Assessment Centers in Japan." *Training & Development Journal*, February 1988.

Taylor, William. "The Logic of Global Business: An Interview with ABB's Percy Barnevik." *Harvard Business Review*, March-April 1991.

Thiederman, Sondra. *Bridging Cultural Barriers for Corporate Success: How to Manage a Multicultural Workforce*. New York: Lexington Books, 1991.

―――. "Managing the Rainbow: Tips on Making it Work." *Cultural Diversity at Work*, November 1991.

Tichy, Noel M., and Stratford Sherman. *Control Your Destiny or Someone Else Will*. New York: HarperBusiness, 1993.

Thurow, Lester C. *Head to Head: The Coming Economic Battle Among Japan, Europe and America*. New York: William Morrow, 1992.

Tixier, Maud. "Management Styles Across Western European Cultures," *The International Executive,* July/August 1994.

Toffler, Alvin. *Powershift: Knowledge, Wealth and Violence at the Edge of the 21st Century*. New York: Bantam, 1990.

Torrington, Derek P., Trevor Hitner, and David Knights. *Management and the Multi-Cultural Work Force*. New York: Gower, 1982.

Townsend, Zachary R. "Leadership in France." American Graduate School of International Management (Thunderbird) research paper, May 13, 1994.

Training. "Industry Report." October 1994.

Treece, James B., Karen L. Miller, and Richard A. Melcher. "The Partners." *Business Week*, February 10, 1992.

Treece, James B. "Ford: Alex Trotman's daring global strategy." *Business Week,* April 3, 1995.

Trompenaars, Fons. *Riding the Waves of Change*. Burr Ridge, IL: Irwin, 1994.

Tuller, Lawrence W. *Going Global*. Burr Ridge, IL: Business One Irwin, 1991.

Tulving, E. "How Many Memory Systems Are There?" *American Psychologist*, 40, 1985.

Tung, Rosalie L. *The New Expatriates: Managing Human Resources Abroad*. New York: Ballinger Publishing, 1987.

————. "Selection and Training of Personnel for Overseas Assignments." *Columbia Journal of World Business*, 16, no.1, 1981.

Tung, R. L., and E. L. Miller. "Managing in the Twenty-first Century." *Management International Review*, 30, no. 1, 1990.

Vaill, Peter B. *Managing as a Performing Art: New Ideas for a World of Chaotic Change*. San Francisco: Jossey-Bass, 1989.

Vance, C. M., D. Boje, and H. D. Stage. "An Examination of the Cross-Cultural Transferability of Traditional Training Principles for Optimizing Individual Learning." Paper delivered at the International Conference of the Western Academy of Management, Shizuoka, Japan, 1990b.

————. "Global Management Education and Development: An Examination of the Cross-Cultural Applicability of Traditional Training Principles." Paper delivered at the National Conference of the Academy of Management, San Francisco, 1990(a).

Vance, C. M., and M. Sailer. A Glimpse of Human Resource Management Issues in Europe. In Mendenhall and Oddou, eds. *Cases and Readings in International Human Resource Management*. Boston: PWS-Kent Publishing Co., 1990.

Victor, David. *International Business Communications*. New York: HarperCollins Publishers, 1992.

Viola, Joy W. *Human Resources Development in Saudi Arabia*. International HRD, 1986.

Volard, Sam V., Dennis M. Francis, and Frank W. Wagner III. "Underperforming U.S. Expatriate Managers: A Study of Problems and Solutions." *Practising Manager (Australia)*. vol. 8, no. 2, April 1988.

Webber, Boss A. *Time is Money*. New York: Free Press, 1990.

Wederspahn, Gary M. "Working With Interpreters." *Cultural Diversity at Work*, November 1991.

Wedman, J. F., and M. Tessmer. "The Layers of Necessity ID Model." *Performance and Instruction*, 29, no. 41, April 1990.

Weeks, William H., Paul B. Petersen, and Richard W. Brislin. eds. *A Manual of Structured Experiences for Cross-Cultural Learning*. Yarmouth, ME: Intercultural Press, 1985.

Weiler, Nick. "GE Strives to Develop New 'Boundaryless' Technical Leaders." *Training Directors Forum Newsletter*, April 1992.

Whalley, John, and Adrian Ziderman. "Financing Training in Developing Countries: The Role of Payroll Taxes." *Economics of Education Review*, 1990.

"Wharton Rewrites the Book on B-Schools." *Business Week*, May 13, 1991.

Wheatley, Margaret J. *Leadership and the New Science*. San Francisco: Berrett-Koehler, 1994.

Wigglesworth, David C. *Bibliography of International Intercultural Literature*. Alexandria, VA: ASTD, 1989.

Williams, Gerald J. "The Key to Expatriate Success." *Training & Development Journal*, January 1990.

Wolniansky, Natalia. "International Training for Global Leadership." *Management Review*, May 1990.

Worthy, Ford S. "You Can't Grow if You Can't Manage." *Fortune*, June 3, 1991.

Wriston, Walter. *The Twilight of Sovereignty: How the Information Revolution Is Transforming the World*. New York: Charles Scribner & Sons, 1992.

Wurzel, Jaime. *Toward Multiculturalism: Readings in Multicultural Education*. Yarmouth, ME: Intercultural Press, 1988.

Yamaguchii, Ikushi. "A Mechanism of Motivational Processes in a Chinese, Japanese and U.S. Multicultural Corporation: Presentation of 'A Contingent Motivational Model'." *Management Japan*, Autumn 1991.

Yankelovich, Daniel. "Tomorrow's Global Businesses." *The Futurist*, July-August 1991.

Yip, George. *Total Global Strategy*. Englewood Cliffs, NJ: Prentice Hall, 1992.

Zimpfer, Forest, and Robert Underwood. "The Status of International Business Communication Training in the 100 Largest Multinational United States Corporations." Eastern Michigan University Report, 1989.

Zuboff, Shoshana. *In the Age of the Smart Machine: The Future of Work and Power*. New York: Basic Books, 1988.

Index